I wish I could show you,
When you are lonely
or in the darkness,
The Astonishing Light
Of your own Being!
~ Hafiz

CHOOSE AGAIN

*Six Steps
to Freedom*

by

Diederik Wolsak

RPC, MPCP

FEARLESS BOOKS

NAPA • CALIFORNIA

FEARLESS BOOKS

PO Box 4199 • Napa CA 94558

info@fearlessbooks.com

© Copyright 2018

by Diederik Wolsak

Names of clients have been changed throughout the text, with the exception of the Testimonials.

ISBN: 978-1-7321850-0-5

Library of Congress Control Number:
2018940037

Cover Photograph
Diederik Wolsak

Design & Typography
D. Patrick Miller

TABLE OF CONTENTS

FOREWORD

With my wife and professional partner, Diane Cirincione-Jampolsky, I first met Diederik Wolsak in 2001, and we bonded immediately with him. He has taken the principles of Attitudinal Healing and *A Course in Miracles* around the world. His Six-Step Process, lectures, and workshops have helped many people change their lives for the better.

Diederik started the Center for Attitudinal Healing, known as Choose Again, in Vancouver, Canada, and later opened a retreat center, El Cielo, in Costa Rica. It was our honor to spend time at the retreat center in 2012, where we found people from all over the world. We really didn't know what to expect before we arrived, but the work we were exposed to went far beyond anything we might have envisioned. In fact, in the 52 countries that have Attitudinal Healing centers, we have never seen such a clear and effective approach. We were impressed that the staff was able to help people with many different kinds of challenges, including difficult addictions. We found El Cielo to be a remarkable around-the-clock healing center, with the Six-Step Process being the cornerstone of the therapeutic technique.

We had travelled to Costa Rica with the full understanding that we would participate in the center's activities, not merely be passive observers. And indeed, Diederik made it clear that he did not want us to sit idly by or even just give a talk or two.

Instead, he wanted us to become part of the mix—part of the group healing process, the focus of which is learning to see the value of letting go of the self-imposed blocks to love that many of us experience—blocks such as guilt and judgment. Members of the group learn how to apply the Six-Step Process to discover and then correct those blocks. We learn to be responsible for our own happiness, rather than blaming others for our state of unhappiness. We also learn that it is only our own thoughts and attitudes that hurt us, and that forgiving others and ourselves completely is the true key to happiness. We come to understand, in a deep and profound way, that the universe has given all of us the freedom to choose what thoughts and attitudes we put into our minds.

Choose Again teaches that we don't have to go through life feeling like we're a victim of circumstance. Rather, we have full control of how we experience our inner as well as outer lives. We learn that there is a healer inside of us and that we can decide to make a decision to be a love-finder rather than a fault-finder, a giver of love rather than a seeker of love, and to live in a consciousness of giving rather than of getting.

Centers and groups devoted to Attitudinal Healing study its twelve principles, the first of which is: *"The essence of our being is love."* We've always thought that if we could practice just this one principle consistently, we wouldn't need to use the other eleven because in this first principle's application we are also able to recognize that the essence of everyone else's being is love, too. Diederik's process reminds us how powerfully healing this principle is.

Diederik's work helps us understand that life is about choices—both conscious and unconscious—and if we're not happy with the choices we've made along the way, we can always forgive ourselves and choose once again.

If there is something in your life that's not working, if you sense an emptiness, a lack of purpose, if you continue to be anxious and fearful, if you're still hurt about the past and fearful of the future, and if you've reached a point in your life where you say to yourself, "There has to be a better way," then this book was meant for you.

It is with great enthusiasm that Diane and I recommend it to you; treat it with utmost respect—for it has the power and the potential to truly change your life.

GERALD JAMPOLSKY, M.D.
Founder of Attitudinal Healing
Co-Author of *A Mini Course for Life;*
Change Your Mind, Change Your Life

INTRODUCTION

*"There is no other way out of misery, which you have created
for yourself through blind acceptance without investigation.
Suffering is a call for enquiry, all pain needs investigation.
Don't be too lazy to think."* ~ NISARGADATTA

✓ Do you pour yourself a stiff drink or a glass of wine
every night to unwind from a stressful day at work?

✓ Is your current marriage beginning to look a lot like
your last?

✓ Do you find yourself stuck in the same rut over and
over again?

✓ Does anger seem to flash up within you, seemingly
on its own?

✓ Does "real" life seem to be passing you by?

✓ Are you numb from taking antidepressants?

✓ Do you seem to have "everything" yet feel an emptiness,
and a nagging sense that something's missing?

If you answered "yes" to any of these questions, then this book
is for you. Happiness is your birthright, and now is a good time
to claim it.

If not now, when?

I have no 'reason' to be happy and yet I am—I am 'unreasonably' happy. Scarred from a childhood most would consider traumatic, most of my adult years were dedicated to self-loathing and self-destruction. The first three and a half years of my life I had been starved of the most basic needs: healthy food, clean drinking water, baths, medical checkups, safety and security. That I survived at all is remarkable. How I managed to create a (relatively) normal, (reasonably) well-adjusted, and happy life now is the subject of this book—for I had to discover how to be happy in order to overcome the chronic rage that characterized the first fifty years of my life. I developed the Choose Again Six-Step Process out of necessity, for my own healing and survival, and I have shared it with numerous grateful clients over the years. It is now yours to use if you choose to do so.

This book shows you how to use this transformational technique to attain inner joy and peace in your own life whatever your circumstances, by first identifying and then removing barriers to love, joy, and lasting peace—regardless of the stories, symptoms, and diagnoses that you now claim as your own.

By reading this book and applying the Choose Again Six-Step process, you can expect to:

- Embark on a journey of self-discovery
- Identify and release thought patterns that no longer serve you
- Banish shame & blame
- Relinquish the victim position once and for all
- Free yourself of your unconscious beliefs
- Nurture inner peace and serenity
- Enrich the quality of your life

- Transform your life for good
- Experience the freedom that comes from taking 100% ownership of your life

One of the foundational premises of this process is that "nothing outside of me can bring me anything I need, and nothing outside of me needs to change in order for me to be happy." Once we realize this, we can get to work examining the barriers to this awareness—the barriers to love that we have created as self-defense. As a result of these barriers we may feel depressed and withdrawn, or we may be addicted to various chemical substances, or may be suffering from any of a number of maladies or conditions. The Choose Again Six-Step Process allows us to remove these barriers to love—barriers that we ourselves have constructed—and in so doing, find the deep inner peace, which every one of us, whether we realize it or not, are always seeking.

This method is highly effective in treating a whole roster of "problems"—including chronic anxiety, depression, addictions, and phobias. It works with the underlying causes rather than with the symptoms, which sets it apart from most other healing techniques, such as behavior modification. Building upon a foundation of Transpersonal Psychology, this healing modality is powerfully augmented by deep spiritual teachings from the major religions. Its principles also draw upon mystics such as Buddha, Lao Tzu, Rumi and Meister Eckhart, as well as current-day teachers: Ramana Maharshi, Poonja, Eckhart Tolle, Jerry Jampolsky, Nisargadatta and Marianne Williamson, to name just a few.

The essence of all of these teachings is based on the same foundational premise, which is: "I am the author of my experience, and everything in my life is for me, it has been chosen by me in order to bring healing." That means that I always have to accept total ownership of my experience, because I have chosen it and all its conditions. In Buddhism, this foundational teaching is expressed differently, although the gist remains the same: "Your life is a dream and you are the author of the dream." Once you accept the possibility that this statement just might be true, then the next step of that authorship is to choose to dream a different dream. You can always choose again.

Chapter One describes my journey from the jungles of Indonesia, where I spent my first three and a half years in Japanese concentration camps, to the jungle in Costa Rica where my healing center is located. I will show you how I constructed the self that I loathed, and how I was able to deconstruct it and in doing so rediscover happiness.

Chapters Two and Three answer the questions "Who do you think you are?" and "Who are you in Truth?" respectively. Chapter Four describes the Choose Again Six-Step Process in its entirety —a process that is applied to any upset, however small, to find out who it is you think you are and correct that mistaken idea by reaffirming the truth of your existence.

Chapters Five through Ten examine each of the six steps in greater detail, giving examples from clients and staff at the Choose Again retreat centers. Note that all the names have been changed to maintain anonymity.

Chapter Eleven describes some of the ripple effects of using the Six-Step Process in families and how powerful it can be when the whole family understands and encourages this way of thinking.

Chapter Twelve describes some of the ways that the Six-Step Process can be misunderstood or abused if care is not taken.

The Afterword details ways in which the Six-Step Process can be applied to a variety of situations to make the world a better place for everyone.

There is a better way—a better way of thinking that leads to transformational healing. In the same way that it has already helped thousands of people to attain inner joy and peace in their lives, it is my deep conviction that the Choose Again Six-Step Process will help you as well.

"If your daily life seems poor, do not blame it, blame yourself that you are not poet enough to call forth its riches. We alone are responsible for the gloominess of our lives. The world is grey because of our blandness. If life remains dreary and your surroundings unbearable, the verdict is in: you can't stand yourself! Make the necessary adjustments."
~ RAINER MARIA RILKE

CHAPTER 1

A Journey from Hellion to Healer

*"Perhaps all the dragons in our lives are princesses who are
only waiting to see us act, just once, with beauty and courage.
Perhaps everything that frightens us is, in its deepest
essence, something helpless that wants our love."*
~ RAINER MARIA RILKE

I AM CRAWLING on my hands and knees in the dust. By the
fence on my right, a little ahead of me, is my elder brother
Joost (pron. *yoast*). We get to the gap in the chain-link fence
we've been looking for. Now we get down on our bellies and
crawl under the fence. There are some greens on the other side; it
is our job to find edible weeds to use as supplements to our meager food supplies. I am eager to help, quickly pick a few leaves,
and proudly show these to my brother.

"No" he says gently. "I'll show you what we want." He then
finds a patch of purslane and says: "That is what is really good,
see if you can find more of these."

I pick a few leaves and taste them. The taste is a little sour but
it is the best thing I had ever tasted. With renewed enthusiasm
we continue to harvest this bounty.

I was born in 1942 to Dutch parents living on the island of
Java in Indonesia in a city then called Batavia, when the world

around us was fraught with tension and war. The Japanese had landed on Java, then a colony of Holland, in March of that year; needing resources such as oil, the Japanese were determined to wrest it from Dutch control. Along with other terrified residents, my parents and my two-year-old brother fled south of what is now Jakarta into the mountains. It must have been a terrifying time. My mother was five months pregnant with me. They had to leave all their earthly goods behind, and their entire social structure was ripped apart. All sense of security, of belonging, of having a 'home' was destroyed overnight.

In July I was born in Pengalengan, a very small hamlet just South of Bandung, on the island of Java. For a brief while my parents and their young son Joost enjoyed the temporary security and beauty of this village, high up in the mountains by a magnificent lake, where the air was refreshingly cool after the sauna-like environment of Jakarta. But their days in paradise were numbered. It was not long after, in September, that we were captured by the Japanese. My parents were forcibly separated, and we were incarcerated in separate POW camps. Women and children were in women's camps, men and boys over the age of six in men's camps. Some 170,000 people were incarcerated, and 25,000 of them did not survive the war.

Despite the fact that I was only a few months old when we went into the camps, and three-and-a-half when we finally emerged, I hold many memories of life in the camp. I remember my brother and I finding a way out of the camp by crawling on our bellies, underneath the barbed wire fence—not to escape, but to find nourishment. We snuck out to pick edible plants we could bring back to the camp for our mother to supplement the daily meager ration of a few thin slices of bread and watery soup we were given. My brother somehow knew what we could eat and what we should avoid. I liked the texture of purslane; the small leaves felt like little pillows. My brother's ability to discern what was edible likely contributed to saving our lives, and I developed a deep connection to him. My very life was in his hands and I trusted him explicitly. That trust has never been broken.

Another camp memory is that of a torture pit. Other little boys and I often crawled up to the edge of the pit. One day I remember looking down and seeing a naked woman being whipped with barbed wire. She was whipped raw and bled heavily. There is no possible way she could have survived this torture. When this memory returned to me in a hypnosis session many years ago, I noticed that there were absolutely no feelings connected to the visual memory. I had already built in a defense mechanism that didn't allow me to feel the horrors of my daily environment. The one feeling I did experience in that session was overwhelming fear.

Although my own mother was never physically tortured, as far as I know, the camp served up her own version of hell. She was a very formal woman with high standards of cleanliness, and was accustomed to living a colonial life of comfort with servants. The camp was the very antithesis of luxury. The conditions were appallingly filthy; disease was rampant; our nutritional needs were not met. Dysentery, jaundice, malaria, typhoid fever and even cholera were very common in the camps, as were pneumonia and other respiratory diseases. In addition, people had to contend with vermin, fleas and lice. All of this—combined with the horrors associated with war—made up my mother's world for three and a half years.

When I allow my mind to revisit this scenario from her perspective, I realize that she had been tortured after all—by not knowing if the hell she had been thrust into would ever end, by not knowing if her husband was still alive, by living in filth, by not knowing if her sons would survive, by watching so many of her peers dying or simply giving up. Later I realized that she was so miserable she wanted to die. However, she forced herself to stay alive for the sake of my brother and me—which I unconsciously absorbed into my impressionable young psyche, developing an enormous amount of guilt about it. I believed that I was responsible for her suffering. It would be years before I could recognize and then disassemble this guilt. Among other deeply buried beliefs I held, this guilt covertly sabotaged my ability to be a happy and psychologically healthy adult, to form loving relationship, and to let in love and trust the love of others.

After the bombing of Hiroshima and the Japanese capitulation, three and a half years after our imprisonment, we were due to be released. However, the local Indonesian population had now turned against us, the Dutch oppressors of three hundred years. If we left the camps, our lives would be in danger. Imagine the utterly schizophrenic scenario we then encountered: we had to stay in the camps and to be protected by the very same Japanese camp guards who had been our tormentors.

Eventually we were released and reunited with my father, all of us just clinging to life at that point. When the bombs dropped on Hiroshima and Nagasaki, I was swollen with edema and not expected to live out the week; my father, formerly a strapping man, weighed a mere one hundred pounds, half his normal weight. We were forced to stay in the camps for months after the Japanese surrender, until some semblance of civic order was restored. Upon our release we went to nearby Australia for a short spell to recover, then back to Indonesia, where I lived for the next five years in its war-torn state while it struggled for independence from Holland.

The end of the war brought a new experience: suddenly I had a father who had been a non-entity to me previously, given that I'd been only a couple of months old when we'd entered the camps. My mother once shared that when the first Dutch man entered the camp the kids ran up to him shouting: "A father, a father!"

The beginnings of rage, shame, and abandonment

"...What happens is of little significance compared with the stories we tell ourselves about what happens. Events matter little, only stories of events affect us." ~ Rabih Alameddin

One day, my father, mother, brother and I were walking on a boardwalk crossing a fish pond near Jakarta. I was holding a shiny red metal truck, my first toy. As you can imagine there were not a lot of toys, or birthday or Christmas presents, during the first few years of my life so I treasured this truck. At one point, however, it slipped out of my hands and fell in the water. The water was clear and I could see the truck on the bottom of it. It couldn't have been more than a couple of feet deep, but my father would not go in the water to get it for me. The rage I felt on that occasion has recurred many times. In fact, it became a predominant theme in my life and it wasn't until much later that I discovered the beliefs I had made up at that vulnerable moment. My three-year-old self interpreted my father's refusal to rescue my truck to mean that I was not supported, not loved, not important.

Other circumstances of my early life subsequently led me to similarly erroneous interpretations. We lived in a state of constant fear; the machine gun nests perched on street corner roofs were an ever-present reminder that we were never safe. Violence, real and implied, was part and parcel of everyday life. On my walk to and from school as a six-year-old I had to cross a park. Every day I was met by a group of Indonesian kids waiting for me who wanted to fight simply because I was white. My father's response to this was: "This will make a man out of you" — while our man-servant Umang found a different solution. Umang was an artist. He made beautiful little statues out of clay decorated with brightly coloured seeds. For the challenge I was facing daily he devised a brilliant solution: he carved a Keris, an Indonesia dagger, out of wood. Thus armed, my traversing the park became much easier.

After my family's release from the camps, we lived in a house on the outskirts of Jakarta. In the backyard was a water tank, placed high upon a tower. My brother had discovered that when we climbed the tower we could look down on an outdoor shower. This we began to do with some frequency, given the fact that from this perch we could observe our native, female domestic help in their daily bathing routines. I suppose it could be said that we were young peeping toms (we were five and seven years old). I have no idea how other young boys viewed adult women when they were my age, but I do know that a nude female has always been profoundly intriguing to me! It might just be because I had only seen emaciated women for three and a half years in the camps. Thus, a healthy female body was extraordinarily attractive.

My mother's health had been severely impacted by the years in the camps and when I was about six she developed pleurisy, a life-threatening lung disease. She was hospitalized in Jakarta. My father was not in a position to look after my younger brother and I, given that he worked all day, so we were lodged with friends of my parents. I don't remember where my brother stayed, but I stayed with a prominent Dutch family. The man of the house was president of a Dutch shipping company that served the Far East. It was here that I developed one of my most crippling beliefs: the belief that I can be betrayed and a deeply held belief in sexual shame and guilt.

While staying with my hosts I discovered a new way to satisfy my young peeping tom habits. If I crouched outside the closed bathroom door while the lady of the house was having a bath, I could peer through the keyhole into the bathroom to view her. I was quite pleased with this discovery, as the hostess was a very beautiful woman in her mid-thirties. I spent many a thrilling moment watching her bathe.

One day I was at the keyhole, so engaged in visual delight that I didn't hear footsteps approaching. All of a sudden, I felt a heavy hand on my shoulder. My father. "What are you doing?" he asked. There might have been a believable explanation for being on my knees with my right eye pressed to the keyhole, but I couldn't come up with anything but "I'm fixing the lock."

What was I thinking? I was busted. My father chose to tell on me, informing the couple what I had been up to. I was kicked out of their house. I never trusted my father again, and I have had many a moment since when an unreasonable fear of betrayal has overwhelmed me. Since that day I've had a huge issue with "tattle-taling" and have a restless radar scanning for betrayal. I felt hugely guilty when I was caught, and that feeling of guilt became an addiction that played out in later events in my life, such as when I was married but fooling around. I came to understand that it is not a symptom such as infidelity that is the real problem for most people, but the underlying cause that must be addressed. The underlying cause in my case was an almost irresistible need, a craving actually, for feelings of guilt, especially sexual guilt.

Another significant memory came during my last few months in Indonesia before being sent to Holland. I had raging night-mares every night, and every night I would scream. My mother would come, comfort me, and I'd fall asleep. On one night I screamed and screamed but she did not come. I crawled out of bed and made my way to the living room where I saw my mother sitting on the couch with a man other than my father, holding hands.

I felt as if I had died.

At that moment I made up another strong core belief: that love can be lost, that I would not be loved, and that I was not lovable.

When I was eight I was sent to Holland and placed in foster care, where I was subjected to minor sexual abuse. The son of the house had tendencies towards boys, and stole the few art supplies my parents had sent with me to Holland. I had to write my parents once a week and in the first letter to my parents, who had remained in Indonesia, I told them how much I hated the couple I was staying with and how desperately unhappy I was. My foster mother asked to see what I had written; she read it and ripped it up saying: "Let's try that again, shall we?" For two years I couldn't communicate with my parents to tell them what was happening to me.

Isolated from my family and increasingly angry, my self-hatred grew, and I became a bully to be reckoned with. My rage was so intense that I was never hurt in any of the daily fights I got myself into, simply because no one could get near me. While in Indonesia I had had to fight Indonesian kids because I was white. In Holland, however, I was called "nigger" because my skin was dark from eight years in the tropics. In this state, that of a 'monster', I had no other identity—there was simply no room for anything else to flourish and grow. At every recess I fought the entire school, which meant some fifty boys formed a circle and ran at me to take shots.

When I was ten I was returned to my biological family. My parents had returned from Indonesia and my brother had come home from boarding school. Although our family was reunited, I remember family dinners were never without tension. My father drank too much and had a terrible temper, which was totally unpredictable. We would be having dinner and out of the blue one of us would be slapped on the back of the head, or receive a blow on our knuckles with a soup spoon. I was beaten two or three times a week.

For many years, I tended to attract people who had anger issues. I replayed my reaction to my father's anger whenever any-one around me raised his or her voice. Today I know that the pur-pose of attracting these "angry" people is to heal a belief I have made up: that I am not safe, that it is all my fault, that I am guilty. Today anger does not affect me and I am now very rarely even remotely disturbed when confronted with anger.

From self-loathing to nothingness

"The chains that keep you bound to the past are not the actions of another person. They are your own anger, stubbornness, lack of compassion, jealousy and blaming others for your choices. It is not other people that keep you trapped; it is the entitled role of victim that you enjoy wearing. There is a familiarness to pain that you enjoy because you get a payoff from it. When you figure out what that payoff is then you will finally be on the road to freedom." ~ SHANNON ALDER

In Holland when I was twelve, boys played either soccer or field hockey. I took up field hockey, which my brother had played at boarding school. We made a dirt field in the back of our garden where the neighborhood boys would come and play for hours every day. Of the five boys who played there on a regular basis, all eventually played first division and three went on to play for national teams. My brother and I both excelled at the sport and eventually played in the first division in Holland and later on the Canadian National Team. My father never supported us emotionally, nor did he ever say a kind word. Instead, he would comment after every game he watched on Sundays that it had been "useless again."

It is important to note that I didn't play competitive field hockey out of any real joy for the game. Rather I was driven to excel by my underlying belief in profound unworthiness. I hid this pretty well, even from myself. If I could diminish or even humiliate an opponent, I briefly "looked good." Years later I noticed many highly successful clients living out that same kind of story. Many chose to excel at something so no one would see what a failure they believed themselves to be, at a deeply hidden level.

Isolated by self-loathing, I became a seeker. Some small part of me desperately needed to know: Other than this vile creature, what else is in me? What is the point? Why was my world the way that it was? Having no one to turn to, no trusted adult by my side, I devoured a world of books for the answers. By the time I was sixteen or seventeen I'd read everything I could get my hands on: Schopenhauer, Nietzsche, Camus, Sartre—you name it, I read it. I read everything and everyone, and every time I'd open a new book and start reading, I'd think, "Wow, this is incredible!" only to become disillusioned shortly thereafter. There were no real answers for me in the books I read, nothing practical that I could apply to my life to help me figure it out, nothing that led in a consistent fashion towards a reasonable understanding of what this life is all about.

Then one night, in the midst of this internal chaos, I awoke in a state of unspeakable peace, joy, and clarity. I had seen something in this state—something I had been deeply searching for. I had seen the answer to my question.

The answer was that there was no question.

I lay back down in bed, determined to return to the state I had awakened from because I wanted to see what this actually looked like. Lying back down, I went back to that blissful state and saw crystal clear blackness: an unspeakable emptiness full of certainty and beauty and infinite peace. It was also a place where I understood—where I *knew* by experiencing the interconnectedness of all things, myself included.

Many years later when I related this experience to a Buddhist Rinpoche, he laughed and laughed. Buddhists have a habit of laughing at just about anything, so I was not taken aback. He then said: "You are a Sunyata Buddha." My ego was quite pleased with that label, but I had no idea what he was talking about, so I asked him what it meant. He said: "It means nothing. It means you have been to Nirvana, but you will never go back there unless you do the work."

Now I know that state of unspeakable beauty and peace is who I really am, and it's who you are too. This absolute clear nothingness is the very essence of our being.

I did not share this experience with anyone. If I'd lived in India, I would have informed a guru and no doubt he would simply have chuckled and said, "Congratulations, you're enlightened," before meandering, nonplussed, on his way. Instead I was sent to psychiatrists and psychologists in what turned out to be one fruitless appointment after another. These well-meaning professionals suffered through the sessions without me ever saying a word. I was stone cold silent. I would not respond to their thoughtful questions, I would not play with toys that were meant to reveal some deeply held disorder to the therapist, I would not participate in any way.

A number of psychotic episodes subsequently ensued, which I shared with no one. I recognized that I was, indeed, going insane —and decided not to allow my mind to "think" anymore. It was simply too dangerous to walk this path without a guide. I am extremely grateful that those years of my journey didn't trans-pire in the 1980s or later, when I would have received so many diagnoses that I would have been medicated into oblivion. PTSD, ADHD, Borderline Personality Disorder, Bi-Polar, Schizophrenia, Autism, Asperger's... these are just some of the labels I could have been stuck with, and would still wear today. I certainly wouldn't have escaped a bewildering array of psycho-tropic medications.

Increasingly isolated, I began to find relief in playing hours of highly competitive sports every day, indulging in alcohol and later, drugs, trying to kill the hateful creature I believed myself to be. Yet I was also trying to rediscover the mysterious experience for which I had no context. Like most addicts, my substance abuse had these two contradictory aspects: self-destruction and misdirected seeking.

But soon the tipping point had been passed and the down-ward spiral of my journey began. As I descended into a hell of my own making, I fell farther and farther away from that spark-ling void of eternal essence that I had known, for a few brief moments, to be my real Self.

Discovering a better way

In 1964, when I was twenty-two, I immigrated to Canada. There I was selected for the Canadian National field hockey team and played internationally for a few years. I attended the University of British Columbia in Vancouver. The initial plan was to study commerce, return to Holland, and join the bank my great-grandfather had founded which, at that time, was still a "family bank." Instead, I switched to fine arts and then architecture, got married in 1969, had two wonderful daughters and embarked on a career as an entrepreneur. I had a landscaping company and worked as a landscape architect, a restaurant owner, and a developer. In each case my business would initially thrive, then my 'belief guided' self-sabotaging tendencies would deliver evidence to prove that I could not and should not succeed. I was married twice and divorced twice. My very strong belief that I was unlovable combined with an enduring conviction that love can, and will, be lost. I would sabotage many relationships before I finally began really healing that belief.

Around the time of my fiftieth birthday, my life was desperately in need of a U-turn if I was to survive. I was drunk every night, and I had determined that unless I could discover a better way, I would drive my car off the road on the Vancouver to Whistler Highway. The drop was several hundred feet, the chances of survival nil.

So I set out, once again, on the path to an awareness of my real Self and, in so doing, arrived back at the place where I had never actually traveled from to begin with. That place is the Truth of who I am, also the Truth of who you are, unchangeably whole and complete. In a pivotal moment of insight, I realized that maybe, just maybe—there might be a way out of my misery. There might be a better way of living after all.

"Here is Edward Bear, coming downstairs now,
bump, bump, bump, on the back of his head, behind
Christopher Robin. It is, as far as he knows, the only way
of coming downstairs, but sometimes he feels that there really
is another way, if only he could stop bumping for a moment
and think of it. And then he feels that perhaps
there isn't." ~ A.A. MILNE

Finding that "better way" took me on a year of intensive study and meditation, and very little else. During that time, I focused on the nature of my self-hatred. Where had it come from? How had I constructed a creature so heinous? In the process of figuring out how I had constructed my self-loathing, I was, of course, beginning to deconstruct it. And that's the process we use today in the profoundly healing work of "Choose Again." This process will help you to deconstruct the identity you made up about yourself at a very young age because, in the vast majority of cases, that formative identity is the source of chronic unhappiness.

We all make up an identity, of which the cornerstone is typically guilt. I made up a 'guilty identity' and you probably did too. Until you realize this and 'own' it with unwavering clarity, you will think that the source of your unhappiness is something outside of yourself. You will think "it's my parents," or "it's the economy," or your boss, partner, or kids. Regardless, it will seem to be someone or something outside of you that needs to change—not you.

Or if you suspect you really are the problem, you'll be tempted to conclude that the situation is hopeless. A psychiatrist I saw in the '70s gave me this encouraging diagnosis on my second (and last) visit: "You are hopelessly eccentric; you'll just have to learn to live with it." Hopeless: an unchangeable identity and character.

As I began to really examine my life, I realized that in order for me to begin deconstructing the self I loathed, I had to learn to feel. In the beginning that was a huge challenge because I only had two feelings: numbness and rage, with very little in between. What I used early on in my process is a "Feeling Sheet," on which are listed nearly seventy different feelings (you'll find it in Appendix A). This feeling sheet allowed me to begin to identify what I was really feeling at any given moment of the day. As a result, I was able to recognize feelings of abandonment, I could isolate feelings of disappointment, and I could identify feelings of rage, fatigue, and hopelessness.

Then I took the next step of accepting the teaching that I was choosing a particular feeling in a particular moment, based on an erroneous core belief that I held about myself. I hope you can hear how important this is:

I choose the feelings I experience. I choose the feelings I experience!

Let that sink in for a minute or so. Let's put it another way: it's my beliefs about myself, my self-made identity, which chooses my feelings. There is no one else in here choosing my feelings for me. So, I had to learn to experience feelings. To do this, I would train my mind to focus on the feeling, and then I'd make it really big. And then I'd say, "Okay, what belief am I holding about myself in this moment that is choosing this particular feeling?" Once I'd been able to isolate and articulate a belief, I'd continue by saying, "That belief is not true. The Truth of me is Love." The Truth does not 'choose feelings' but automatically engenders a state of being which can be called bliss. That's a given. If I were in my True mind, I'd be 'in love'. There would be no anger, or sadness, or envy. And that is because in Truth, there is only an experience of unconditional Love.

By observing all of my feelings, I was able to uncover the deeply held beliefs about who I thought I was that were driving my behavior. As I learned to recognize the insanity of those beliefs and correct them by replacing them with the knowledge of who I truly am, my behavior changed accordingly. With the help of a group of counselors in Vancouver, I began to put together a practical way of incorporating the lessons I'd learned from spiritual texts (see the Recommended Reading list in Appendix D), utilizing the principles of Attitudinal Healing. When I became a professional counselor I formalized this process into the Choose Again Six-Step Process.

The result was the establishment of the Choose Again Attitudinal Healing center in Vancouver, with the opening of a residential center in Costa Rica a few years later. Living at the center near Arenal in Costa Rica provides me with an opportunity to continue to work on myself every day, while at the same time holding up a mirror reflecting the Truth to others to recognize their own true Self.

I'm increasingly less tolerant of a feeling or a state of being other than joy or peace. I'm increasingly losing all fascination with the thoughts that cause upsets. For instance, I don't find it particularly interesting to be angry anymore. I used to get a perverse sense of false power from anger, and I was good at it. But I don't find it interesting anymore. I don't find sadness interesting anymore. I don't get off on sad stories. They simply don't touch me.

What moves me now is love.

People come to me with heart-wrenching stories of trauma, of sexual abuse, of emotional abuse. I listen to them but I don't react. And at the end of the story the bearer of it will ask me, perplexed, "Doesn't any of that touch you?"

"Well no, it doesn't touch me," I respond, "because it doesn't reflect the truth of who you really are. Your story has nothing to do with who you really are. The truth of who you really are is what moves me. I get teary-eyed when you and I connect at that true level, when we connect with love. Then I cry. But your story won't make me cry because your story is not you. It is just a story."

The only reason to tell the story of my early years is to demonstrate unequivocally that whatever happened to you and me when we were young does not have the power to keep us prisoner for life. I have seen too many people recover from un-speakable early life trauma, people who had been told they would never 'get over' their past.

My story is not who I am, either. It led me to believe that I was a monster, but that is not who I truly am. I was fortunate enough to experience my true Self when I was a teenager, and that knowledge kept me from completely self-destructing, and it eventually led me back to my Self. I know the truth of who you really are, because that is the Truth for both you and me. In the following chapters I'll show you how your current identity came about. Then we'll begin the work of deconstructing it, which will enable you to connect to profound inner peace and contentment.

"Paths are made by walking," said Franz Kafka. The paths we are making by inner processing of our feelings and beliefs are new neuropaths. We are actually changing our minds at the deepest levels. Compare this to making a path through a rainforest, a very dense and entangled environment. It takes hard work, but after a lot of sweating and slashing and cursing we have our path.

Now, what do you think happens if you stopped there? What

would that path look like in a month? There would be no path anymore; the rainforest would swallow it up, just like the ego can swallow up all effect of a few well-meaning Six-Step Processes. You have to keep the way open; you have to keep processing till that tentative little path has become a six-lane highway, and even then you'll have to maintain it. Like a rainforest, the ego simply waits for you and I to slack off. Are you worth it? Are you worth the sustained, committed and disciplined approach to changing your mind?

CHAPTER 2

Who Do You Think You Are?

*"The closer you come to knowing that you alone create
the world of your experience, the more vital it becomes for
you to discover just who is doing the creating."*
~ ERIC MICHA'EL LEVENTAHL

WHO IS doing the creating? You are. I am. But not the One
we are in truth. Who is creating my experience is the
creature I made up—but that creature has become a
rogue robot.

The 'I' you think you are may have thoughts like these:

- *"In the eyes of the world, I'm a very successful lawyer, but at home I'm angry all the time."*
- *"I'm a teacher who loves to read in my spare time. I have a perfect job, I am just so depressed, nothing seems to really matter."*
- *"I'm a lousy wife and mother—I can't seem to do anything well enough."*
- *"I'm the life and soul of every party, but I don't have any really good friends."*

When someone you have just met asks you about yourself,
you may tell them about your job, your interests, and your family.

We tend to define ourselves by our position in society, our education, our favorite sports teams, our hobbies. Our doctors might define us by our health issues; our accountants by how much money we have. We are labeled, categorized, and defined in many different ways.

Society has encouraged us to project an outward image that is often at odds with what we feel inside. We strive to look good, dress well, display the trappings of a chosen style, and possess the gadgets and status symbols that will allow us to be judged favorably by our neighbors. This obsession with appearance is the result of having lost touch with who we really are. We do not want anyone to see who we think we really are, so we are constantly on guard to hide the aspects of ourselves we despise.

There is a subconscious part of our identity made up of core beliefs, many of which may be hidden from our own view. Nonetheless, this collection of beliefs drives our behaviors, and literally chooses our feelings and our experiences for us. This is the small "s" self, or ego. This set of beliefs is what I actually believe I am.

Many of us are not even aware that our minds have made up a "self" that is running the show and wreaking havoc in our lives. If you recognize a pattern of behavior in your life—finding yourself in some kind of frustrating situation over and over again—you can be sure that pattern is driven by subconscious beliefs. The good news is that by becoming aware of those beliefs and bringing them to light, you can transform your behavior patterns. This is how addictions are healed, chronic stress is relieved, and depression becomes a memory.

In order to begin to do the work necessary to become truly happy, we must first get a clear idea of who we think we are. This chapter will show how the ego develops—the self that we "think" we are, based on unrecognized core beliefs.

The Development of Core Beliefs

For most of us, our parents looked at us with pure love and absolute delight when we were born. They cuddled and comforted us, fed us, changed us, and marveled at every new stage in our development. We were perfect in their eyes.

As children we are totally egocentric—we automatically assume that the world is entirely about us. Adoring parents give us the message that not only are we safe and taken care of, we are inherently worthwhile and deserving of love.

But there comes a point, sooner or later when something happens, and a parent or caretaker reacts to us in a way that is less than loving. Perhaps Mom had a difficult day and reacts with irritation when we throw food from the high chair, or maybe Dad comes home drunk. Having known only loving parents before, we now experience uneasiness, and assume that we must have done something to cause this new and unexpected behavior by a parent. Our young mind will always assume that it is our fault. How many times did our mother or father say: "You make me so happy"? It stands to reason that if I, as a baby, can make an adult happy, then I can also cause their unhappiness.

When mom gets angry again, or dad comes home drunk for the third or fourth time, we will use this additional evidence to cement a belief that we are bad, unworthy, unlovable, destined to be a victim—or any one of a number of negative beliefs. This can include the assumption that if we were truly lovable, dad would not drink and mom would never be irritated. Sounds a little insane, doesn't it? And, yet, that is how we all formed what we now call our 'personality' or 'character.'

Once such a belief is firmly established, we will begin to look at the world through the lens of that belief. If we believe we are bad, we will keep a record of every time we are scolded or punished in some way, while we must overlook the many times we had fun with our parents. We must overlook those memories because in order to preserve and strengthen the beliefs I hold about myself, I cannot allow contradictory evidence to enter my awareness. "No one can convince you of a truth you do not want," says *A Course in Miracles*. Through the lens of our beliefs, we will focus on the things that seem to go wrong, and all the ways we are treated badly or unfairly.

Any core belief demands evidence to be sustained. So we will behave in such a way that the necessary evidence will be supplied. For instance, we may subconsciously provoke the anger of a parent, the irritation of a teacher, being left out by our group of friends. These events will produce the feeling of shame and rejection that the core belief requires to maintain its hold.

In other words, the deeply buried belief that there is something 'shameful' about who I am will direct me to act in ways that elicit that feeling.

This feedback loop shown in the illustration on the next page strengthens the beliefs which coalesce to form our identity. And that core belief will remain in control of every aspect of your life until you learn that it can be challenged and transformed.

Young children typically assume that it is somehow their fault if their parents get a divorce. If we were accustomed to hearing our parents telling us, "You make me so happy," then when they were not happy, we will conclude that somehow it was our fault they weren't happy. Now there may have been parents who were happy all the time, but I have not had the pleasure of meeting any! We all made up a belief that we were responsible for our parents' happiness, and later in life, that we are responsible for our partner's happiness. One definition of relationship hell is to hold yourself responsible for your partner's happiness.

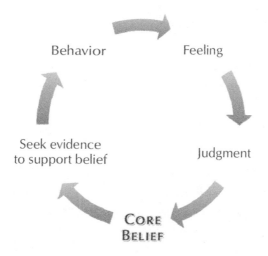

When my first daughter was born, I was drunk in the delivery room. However, when I laid eyes on my new little girl, I thought, *She's the most incredible thing I've ever seen!* and *I'm going to stop drinking because I want to be there for her.*

But I didn't stop drinking.

What's the core belief she might have developed as a result of having a father who was an alcoholic? I'm NOT the most incredible thing he's ever seen. There's something wrong with me, otherwise he would stop drinking. I have learned that every child of alcoholic parents has this belief. The fact that I wouldn't give up drinking at that time, even for my beautiful daughter, provided further evidence for my own core beliefs that I was worthless, monstrous, and weak. As a matter of fact, the self I had made up could not afford to stop drinking. It is not possible to go against a core belief; the belief will ultimately win.

Every single one of us has made up some limiting core beliefs about ourselves, and it's these beliefs that run (or ruin) our lives today—without us even being aware of them! Some core beliefs common to most people are:

- *I'm not loved (or "lovable")*
- *I'm not important*
- *I don't matter*
- *I'm not supported*
- *I have nothing to offer*
- *Whatever I do will be wrong, it will never be enough*
- *I deserve to be punished—I'm bad*
- *I can lose love*
- *I'm not good enough*
- *There is something seriously wrong with me*
- *I'm guilty*
- *I'm a victim*

These and other beliefs were made up by me and you at an early age, as a result of how we interpreted certain things that occurred—people spoke to us in a particular tone of voice; there was conflict; perhaps some drama ensued—and this chain of events had an impact on our young and impressionable minds.

The Red Truck Cycle

In my own life, there are still times when I feel a rage welling up if I perceive that I am not supported. This can happen at a meeting if support seems to be lacking for one of my ideas; when my partner does not agree with a statement I just made; when a business partner asks for a few more days to consider my proposal. I have traced this back to an incident that occurred fairly shortly after the war, mentioned earlier: my father's refusal to retrieve my precious red truck, which I had accidentally dropped into a pond. He didn't seem to care how much the truck meant to me, and I interpreted his reaction to mean that I was not supported, not loved, and at the deepest level, worthless.

This cycle of belief formation and the subsequent evidence it demands is illustrated in the following diagram:

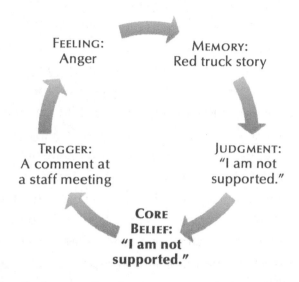

FEELING: Anger

MEMORY: Red truck story

JUDGMENT: "I am not supported."

CORE BELIEF: "I am not supported."

TRIGGER: A comment at a staff meeting

The anger I might feel in response to a comment at a staff meeting is the same anger I felt toward my father years ago. The bad news about the core belief—I'm not supported—is that it demands evidence, so I will subsequently behave in a way that will show me how bad, worthless, or unlovable I am. So even if I am supported I will think that I'm not. Or worse, I will reject any support that comes my way. I will sabotage the respect or love that's being offered until it is finally withdrawn, and then I'll say: "See, I knew it!"

Fortunately by now I have mostly healed that belief of not being supported, and I have also trained my mind to catch any feelings of rage as they arise. When they do, I immediately process the mistaken belief that I'm not supported. I've been the fortunate recipient of astonishing levels of support all my life, but only in the last twenty years or so have I learned to allow this love and support to be an integral part of my life.

There is an interesting side note to the red truck story. While recently having dinner with my elder brother Joost, he shared some memories from our days in Indonesia. He then told a story about dropping his red truck into the fish pond—exactly as I have told it! I looked at him with amazement and said: "That's truly remarkable, that is my story. I have told and retold this story in workshops for years. I never heard it from you."

So what actually did happen? We will never know. Either it happened how he remembered it—it was his truck that fell in the water and I took on his rage —or vice versa. It doesn't matter. Regardless, I developed a destructive belief based on that incident and I played out that belief for a long time. It is so important to realize that whether a memory is based on fact or is purely of my own imagination is not important. In my mind it happened and I suffer from the made-up memory because I have made it real.

Tracing upset feelings to core beliefs formed in our past is the method employed by the Choose Again Six-Step Process. This link between our feelings and our memories has been well documented by Joe Dispenza in his book *You Are the Placebo*. By investigating the memories that are linked to feelings, we can discover the beliefs that were generated at that time. Once a belief is uncovered and exposed as merely a belief, the barriers to happiness begin to dissolve. However, if a belief is left unrecognized and unchallenged, it will persist, produce more evidence of its validity, and become stronger and stronger, cementing a fortress defending against love or joy.

Should I have been born?

Let's look at another personal example. In Chapter 1, I discussed my life in the concentration camp in Indonesia, and how

I sensed that my mother wanted to die but stayed alive for my brother and I. Sixty-five years later, I am at our healing center in Costa Rica on a day when absolutely everything is going wrong. And not just a little bit wrong, completely off-the-rails wrong. I felt as though everything was crashing down around me and I just wanted to crawl into a hole and die. This was a very power-ful feeling, one I wasn't familiar with. I asked myself, "What's the message of this powerful feeling?"and the message was: *I shouldn't have been born.* Now I had heard that belief expressed by others about themselves, but I had never recognized it as a belief of my own.

And yet there it was.

I realized that I needed to do some work to identify the core belief that was making me feel so miserable. I couldn't access the memory that produced it, so I did Holotropic breathing, a highly effective transformational tool that we use at the Choose Again centers. Rapid, strong in-breaths over a prolonged period of time (with trained supervision) induce a highly oxygenated brain, which produces a state in which one's normal defenses are bypassed, often allowing deeply suppressed subconscious thoughts to surface.

What was eventually revealed was that I had deep feelings of guilt associated with my mother. The sheer strength of the guilt feelings indicated that I had hurt her in some horrible way. I know I had hurt her in the small ways that typically happen with normal family dynamics, but this motherlode of guilt was much deeper, and disproportionate to the circumstances of our early relationship.

Or so I thought.

What my breath work revealed was that my mother wanted to die in the camp because it was utterly unbearable. The only reason she didn't was to ensure that my brother and I would survive. Thus I had "hurt her very deeply" for a number of years, although we actually did nothing but survive. This realization made sense, and I could process it quickly. The belief that I had felt so strongly, however, was that I should never have been born!

How could I have gotten that message? I got it from my guilt as a child, but I also got it from the fact that my mother had been pregnant with me when she, my father and my brother were fleeing the Japanese, traveling into the mountains in order to escape the invaders. What was the message I had picked up energetically in utero from my mother? This is not a great time to be pregnant. You can see how this "double whammy" of similar beliefs combined to create the debilitating conviction that I had about myself. It lay buried in my psyche, waiting for just the right moment to surface, which it did on that day at the Center sixty-five years later. This happens with all beliefs; they will all surface sooner or later.

Guilt: The Common Denominator

Guilt is found in the psyche of everyone on the planet, and from it springs all manner of other erroneous beliefs that run our lives. Let's consider the justice system. In North America, there exists the largest jail population per capita of any society in the history of mankind. I would argue that every single person in jail has a strong underlying belief that they are guilty.

Now you might say, "Well they are guilty. They stole, they murdered, they committed arson," and so on. My response would be, "Yes, they did all those things but why did they do them? They did them in order to get evidence for the belief that they're guilty." In other words, the belief that they are guilty preceded their criminal behaviors. Some 1800 years ago Augustine of Hippo saw this play out early in his life with incredible clarity:

> *"Behold, now, let my heart tell you what it was seeking there, that I should be gratuitously wanton, having no inducement to evil but the evil itself. It was foul, and I loved it. I loved to perish. I loved my own error— not that for which I erred, but the error itself. Base soul, falling from Your firmament to utter destruction— not seeking anything through the shame but the shame itself."*

"Not seeking anything through the shame but the shame itself..." Do you identify with this insight? If we have a strong belief in our guilt we're going to find a way to express it. Whether it means being unfaithful to our partner, running our business in such a way that we'll be saddled with a huge lawsuit, or getting into major debt and having to declare bankruptcy—whatever it is, we're going to find evidence for our guilt.

When people come to a healing circle and explain why they are there, the symptoms vary. Typically there will be someone with treatment-resistant depression or a substance abuse issue, someone who's dropped out of university because they didn't get good grades, and another person who is wondering how to keep her second or third marriage together. All of them have the same issue—a deep sense of self-hatred, a strong belief in guilt, or self-hatred based on guilt—even though the presenting symptoms are different. Whether this self-hatred takes the form of depression, chronic stress, alcohol, philandering or overworking makes no difference. The symptom is never the issue.

Belief in guilt is universal. Underneath every upset is guilt; underneath every twinge of sadness is guilt; underneath every expression of grief is guilt. I believe there's not a single person who doesn't have a low-grade, constant sense of chronic guilt.

We all do. The questions we need to face about it are:

1. Am I aware of my belief in my guilt?
2. Where does this guilt come from?
3. How and when did I make this up?

The last question is connected to an even deeper one: Why do we ALL feel guilty? That has a simple if not obvious answer: Guilt finds its genesis in the belief that we're no longer part of the Oneness—the Oneness that is Truth, the Oneness that is wholeness, the Oneness that is only Love. We feel that we are no longer part of this divine Oneness and so we must have done something to be kicked out of the Club of One. The primary guilt I feel is simply because the 'self' I invented is in direct contradiction to the truth of my 'Self'. This topic will be discussed more fully in Chapter 3.

Core Beliefs and Addiction

When people come to see us with an addiction, they typically want to talk about being addicted to substances. However, substances are never the issue. The substances are just the tip of an iceberg of feeling. We may feel long-standing tension in our body; we may feel desperately lonely; we may be chronically anxious or worried, or we may get angry at the drop of a hat. These are feelings. Feelings have a bio-chemical component and we are addicted to these bio-chemicals. That's how we become addicted to these feelings.

Where do these feelings come from? Our feelings are chosen by the beliefs we have about ourselves. If I have a belief that I'm not supported, I will find evidence to show I'm not being supported. When I see that evidence in any form, I will feel rage, and it is that feeling of rage that I am addicted to. In this vicious cycle, I became addicted to the feeling of rage associated with the idea that I am not supported (see diagram).

We can begin to understand the roots of our addictions to feelings, and to substances, when we can answer the question "Who do you think you are?" Thus, the key to unraveling our deep sadness, depression, substance abuse, workaholism, eating disorders, and other debilitating "symptoms" is to tackle the underlying belief structure that makes up who we think we are. This has been the key to the remarkable success Choose Again has enjoyed, working with clients with all kinds of presenting issues, whether it be depression, stressed relationships, chronic anxiety or substance abuse. The Six-Step Process is the method by which this dismantling of core beliefs can be achieved.

Before I committed to my own healing work, my alcohol intake was substantial. I was drunk almost every night for about thirty years. This abuse was purely a choice I made based on my deep sense of self-hatred. This self-hatred was the outcome of a set of core beliefs that included my being unlovable, guilty, worthless, and deserving of punishment. These beliefs demanded evidence which my alcoholic behaviour amply supplied.

I went to Alcoholics Anonymous for help and learned their perspective on the issue: Alcoholism is an illness and I, as an alcoholic, am powerless over it. I believed this for a while. After having worked on myself using the Choose Again methodology, I came to understand that it's the ego which believes it's powerless over alcohol (and many other things). Now I would never say that I'm powerless over anything. This is because I've learned that who I am in Truth—beyond the ego—is infinitely powerful, not powerless.

AA has helped many people and I admire its record. It's a

magnificent organization that's saved literally millions of lives and continues to do so. And, yes, it could go further. Many AA veterans who have been at our Center stated with surprise: "This is the missing link!" A key question needs to be asked: "Why was I drinking in the first place? Where did that come from?" If you're drinking too much you need to ask yourself, "What's the purpose of my drinking? What is its function? What do I get to be right about when I drink?" It's the urgency and necessity of drinking that needs to be addressed. This urgency and necessity is informed by an underlying belief that makes me want to destroy the 'self' I hate.

In my case, not only was I drinking too much—I was also doing drugs, philandering, and sabotaging my business on all levels. I was trying to self-destruct. I did not succeed. Sadly, some people do succeed, or remain on a self-destructive treadmill.

Why did I drink so much? For two reasons: one, I was on a misguided search for a higher self through a transcendent experience. In my self-styled fanaticism I thought booze was going to take me there—it would transport me to that spiritual realm I was seeking (is it just a coincidence that alcohol is called "spirits"?).

The second reason I drank was to destroy the self I hated so much. Why didn't that work? Because it can't be destroyed. I was trying to destroy a belief—the belief in my worthlessness —but you can't actually destroy a belief. What you can do is withdraw your attachment to it. Take away the faith in your own belief, and it will wither. With it will go your self-destructive feelings and behaviors.

Here's a diagram of my drinking belief cycle:

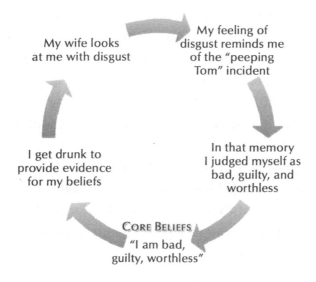

Fixing Symptoms Doesn't Work

*"Correction belongs only at the level where change is possible.
Change does not mean anything at the symptom level,
where it cannot work."* ~ A COURSE IN MIRACLES

If you're a drinker and manage to give up alcohol, nothing really happens except that you are not drinking anymore. You have to go to the source, the reason behind the drinking, to truly become free of addiction. Otherwise you'll either go back to drinking, or find other ways to express your self-loathing. Back in 1986 when I attended AA meetings for a few months, I was struck by how many people were smoking. The fact that virtually every treatment facility in North America allows smoking is truly puzzling. What's the difference between smoking and drinking? What is the message I give myself when I light up a cigarette? When you get down to it, they're both expressions of self-hatred.

The Choose Again Six-Step Process tackles underlying beliefs, not symptoms. Addressing the cause of drinking, rather than trying to manage the drinking itself, is the difference between Choose Again and Alcoholics Anonymous. By transforming the roots of the self-loathing that prompts drinking to excess, the motivation for excessive drinking is eliminated and will not be transferred to other destructive behaviors. Having said that, of course, the first thing many people need to do is stop drinking, snorting coke, or whatever behavior their self-hatred compels them to pursue, but that is as far as behavior modification will go in our work. Behaviors are permanently erased only with the removal of their cause.

How do we discover who we think we are?

The Choose Again Six-Step Process is a powerful tool for un-covering the beliefs that make up who we think we are. It uses the feelings experienced in an upset to rediscover a memory of a child-hood incident in which a core belief was generated. Applying this radical process to every upset results in remarkable and remarkably quick transformation and healing.

There are at least three other gateways to accessing and identifying our major beliefs, which I will briefly discuss here. They are our judgments of others, our attachments to things, and our special relationships.

Judgments

When we judge other people critically, we are really seeing the parts of our egos that we don't like. If there is any emotion behind a judgment, we can be sure that it actually applies, in some way, to ourselves. If we are just observing without an emotional involvement, then what we are seeing is less likely to be about us. If I see someone taking the last piece of cake on a dessert tray and I am pissed off, I am looking at an old belief in scarcity: 'there will never be enough for me'. If I look at a birch tree and comment on its grace, it does not mean I have a deeply buried belief that I am a birch tree.

We often resent hearing that the things we hate about others are really attributes that we have ourselves, and do not want to look at. Whenever you feel strongly judgmental, the first thing to do is to ask, "Would I accuse myself of that?" Often you'll have buried that particular fault, trying to portray yourself as its total opposite, because acknowledging that self-judgment is too painful. The next time you want to judge someone, take a long hard look in the mirror and see how that judgment plays out in your own life.

One of our staff members, Charles, had a very powerful fear of being gay. When I asked him "What is your judgment on people who are gay?" he would not express any judgment. Gay people are fine, nothing wrong with them. But that clearly was not the case at a much deeper level. So we went back to the feelings that came up for him when he considered the possibility that he too might be gay. He allowed the feelings to grow, and eventually recognized them as disgusting, monstrous, horrible, something wrong. None of these had anything to do with sexual preference, and everything to do with how Charles saw himself. All these judgments were traced back to a memory of him witnessing his parents arguing, and concluding that it was somehow his fault. Much later, he projected these feelings onto gay people. By processing each of these core beliefs, Charles gained a tremendous sense of peace around this issue. Whether he actually was gay or not no longer mattered at all, and never did!

Attachments

> *"A mind attached to anything becomes a sick weak mind.*
> *A weak mind will keep going to the garbage of attachment*
> *and this causes the nervous system to get squeezed and*
> *weakened so it cannot handle this very energetic decision*
> *for freedom. A strong mind is needed to make the strong*
> *decision and handle the power that will come with it. To heal*
> *disease you must first decide that you want to be free of pain*
> *and suffering. Without wanting this nothing else will work.*
> *To forgive and forget is the best medicine for curing all pain.*
> *Let the thought that causes pain come into the present and*
> *discharge into Emptiness. Do this now!"*
> ~ Sri H.W.L. Poonja

What do you think you couldn't live without? If you're attached to a particular consumer good, like shoes, you may be convinced that you need a new pair of high heels every week in order to feel attractive. This desire is driven by the larger, overarching belief that you need something outside of yourself to be secure or feel happy. Underneath such a belief is likely a deeper one: I am not lovable the way I am, there is something lacking within me.

Special Relationships

A special relationship is one in which each holds the other responsible for how they feel. In a special relationship, I have given my partner the task of making me happy. The arrangement stems from a belief in lack, that what I need has to be supplied by my partner. Finally, a special relationship is a prolonged bargaining session which is doomed to fail; sooner or later my partner does not keep his or her end of the bargain.

Yet ultimately, we attract partners who share our beliefs in order to heal them together.

I used to attract people who had a noticeable addiction to the feeling we call anger. They came into my life in order to offer me a steady stream of replays of my father's anger. What was the purpose of attracting anger? Ultimately it was to heal my belief that I deserve to be punished, and to heal my huge fear that when someone is angry it means I will be abandoned.

My partner will always push my buttons and trigger my beliefs better than anyone else, so if I pay attention to those triggers, we'll both discover the beliefs that we need to heal. Relationships are the most powerful healing laboratories available to us all.

We think we are our labels

In the same way that we hold ideas about who we think we are (introverted, bad at math, a poor driver, phobic about heights), many of us are also labeled with diagnoses such as ADHD, anorexic, bi-polar, or depressed, to name just a few. If we allow ourselves to be labeled and we accept the authority of an outsider to give weight to the label, then inevitably we become the label. I have certainly seen people who were labeled in some way act more and more like the label over time. There is a seductive quality to a label or diagnosis: "I am off the hook. Now I know why I've always behaved the way I do." The label absolves one from taking ownership of a problem or behavioral tendency.

A young woman who was twenty-two, deeply depressed, and on suicide watch came to see me for a session. Her psychiatrist had given her a life sentence: "You'll never be happy!" If she had believed that, where do you think she'd be now? Someone had told her about our work, and she came to see me in Vancouver.

She instantly connected with the suggestion that depression and suicidal ideation were part of a deeper issue and were chosen by her to support some core beliefs about herself. Two days later she was at our center in Costa Rica, and three days later she had commuted her life sentence. She learned that she could choose again; she had a vote after all. Very quickly she decided to shed the labels and start living. It does not always go that quickly; progress depends on how ready someone is to choose again. It depends on how strongly the person wants to be right about something that had happened in the past, and whether one is willing to let everyone in the past off the hook.

Whether you've been labeled as bipolar, depressed, suicidal, or anything else, it's crucial to remember that those labels only point toward symptoms. Those symptoms are informing you that there is something wrong with your belief system; there's something wrong with who you think you are. Your mistaken identity is manifesting as depression, or as manic behavior, or as being habitually conflicted, but that is not who you are. Understanding who we think we are is the prerequisite to transforming our everyday experiences. Getting in touch with who we really are puts us on the path to healing, the subject of the next chapter.

Summary

1) We make up core beliefs about ourselves as young children.
2) Our beliefs demand evidence, which we will find in our everyday activities.
3) Beliefs run like default programs determining our behavior, and creating barriers to happiness. We think we are our beliefs, our stories, and our labels, but none of these are who we really are.

4) Awareness and correction of these beliefs are essential for becoming happier and healthier, by decreasing their power over us.

5) We can find out what our beliefs are by examining our upsets and feelings using the Choose Again Six-Step Process, and by examining our judgments, attachments, relationships, and labels.

Chapter 3

Who You Are In Truth

*"Waves are not separate from the Ocean, rays are not separate
from the Sun, you are not separate from Existence-
Consciousness-Bliss. This is a reflection of That."*
~ Sri H.W.L. Poonja

*"The first peace, which is the most important, is that which
comes within the souls of people when they realize their relationship,
their Oneness with the universe and all its powers, and they realize
that at the center of the universe dwells the Great Spirit, and
that this center is really everywhere, it is within each of us."*
~ Black Elk (Sioux)

I N THE last chapter we saw how we create our little 's' selves
—our ego identities—comprising a collection of beliefs about
our innate guilt and many flaws. But the truth of who we
are is the big 'S' or Higher Self, that has always been there, will
always be there, and simply waits to be noticed and claimed.
Every mystical tradition throughout the ages has a very similar
understanding of this 'Self' as the primordial energy that is connected to everyone and everything else. This Self is eternal and
can never be destroyed. This is our spirit Self. It could be said
that this Self is the Essence of Love.

This chapter will look at the implications for our experience

of 'happiness', our experience in our daily life, when we accept
that Oneness is the Truth of our being. Happiness does not depend
on 'understanding' Oneness because it cannot be understood,
there is no-one outside of this Oneness to do the understanding.

It does depend on the acceptance of the possibility of Oneness. We can learn to think, behave, and relate as if that possibility
has become reality for us.

The foundation of the idea of Oneness is that Self/God/Brah-
man is indivisible, and we are an integral part of that unified
entity. This is the concept known as "nonduality." Nonduality is
the philosophical, spiritual, and scientific understanding of non-
separation and fundamental intrinsic Oneness. The major main-
stream religions tend to appear to espouse duality: God is an
all-powerful 'other' and humans are separate, lesser beings. The
contrasts of Oneness versus duality are enormous, with acceptance
of the idea of Oneness potentially leading to a dramatically more
joyful mindset. Nonduality underlies the Choose Again Six-Step
Process.

Scientifically, it is easy for us to understand the concept of
Oneness in terms of the building blocks of all matter — we are made
up of combinations of atoms and molecules just like everyone
and everything else. We are made up of protons, neutrons and
electrons vibrating in space. In this sense we are naturally a part
of everything always. As Erwin Schroedinger noted, "Quantum
physics reveals a basic Oneness of the universe."

Within the concept of Oneness we are whole and complete.
Within the concept of Oneness there is only Isness, which does
not allow for good or evil, right or wrong, no cause for sadness or
loss. Within this Truth there's no suffering. This is where we can
find our true, unchallenged Joy, by learning to access the magni-
ficence of our higher Selves, by learning to release our attachment

to the ego self. Remember, that small self is nothing more than a set of false beliefs we hold about ourselves.

Earlier I talked about my experience of Oneness when I was a young man, awakening in the middle of the night with a vision of limitless black, crystal-clear space. Words cannot describe the extraordinary peace I felt. If you yourself have ever experienced it, you know exactly what I'm talking about. It's my belief that every one of us has experienced this, if only for a split second: a moment without even a hint of judgment is an experience of Oneness.

Breathing into Oneness

Awareness of Oneness is one of the frequently reported experiences induced by Holotropic Breathwork, a therapeutic technique that is part of the Choose Again methodology.

One of the Choose Again counselors, Ted, explained that his experience during one Holotropic Breathing session confirmed for him that there exists a state of bliss beyond our usual everyday experience, but available to us as a true expression of who we are. "I had an experience of transcendence, to a state of mind not possible in everyday life. It stopped me from arguing and discussing the premise of Oneness used by Choose Again—it was a turning point—I simply couldn't argue with it anymore. I entered a realm of pure light, of which the essence was Love. The intensity was so strong that I couldn't stand it. It may only have lasted a few seconds, but I longed to go back there. It was impossible to be in that state while retaining a separate ego. My longing to go back has turned into deep gratitude for the experience, which was such a gift, rather than lamenting that I am not in that space all the time."

Another client of mine was an older man who was having some issues at work. A Texas oilman from Houston, he was a tough businessman, hard-working and driven to succeed. He couldn't begin to relate to the spiritual aspect of our methodology at all. He was completely against the whole idea of God and while he wanted and needed help, he was very clear in his own mind about the nature of the universe and his place in it. He told me, bluntly: "I'm not into your woo-woo spirituality and don't even talk to me about God. I've never had a belief in God and that's not going to change anytime soon."

My answer to him was, "Well then, we can stop the session, or I could suggest a different process. Would you be interested in that?" Since the gentleman had travelled a long way to meet with me, he said, "Okay, sure." So I told him about Holotropic Breath-work and he agreed to try it. He breathed with a machine-like energy; he breathed and breathed and breathed and nothing was happening. After about 45 minutes of incredibly consistent and hard breathing it occurred to me that, possibly, this process, too, would not benefit him. Then suddenly the tears came. He ended up on the floor, sobbing convulsively on his hands and knees.

This was early in my career and I made the mistake of think-ing that I recognized what happened to him, so I said: "It would seem that a lot of sadness came up for you." He turned to me and he said, "Sadness? Hell no, I was with God!" So there he was, merged with the Oneness, the totality, God—whatever you want to call it. This changed his life, giving him an insight into his own spiritual world and a deep sense of purpose.

When a family with a fourteen-year-old autistic girl visited the center, her mother expressed concern about whether it would be wise for her daughter to participate in a Holotropic Breathing session. I confirmed that we would keep a close eye on her, as we always do, and that she would be safe. She started her breathing and within just a few minutes, she ran out of the room. I followed her, sat on the steps outside and asked her what happened. She said: "I am really, really scared!"

"What is the fear, can you tell me?" I asked.

"I was going far, far away," she replied, "and I was afraid I would never be able to get back."

"Where did you go?"

"I went far away, way past the galaxies."

I am convinced that she experienced a moment of true enlightenment. "Way past the galaxies" isn't that another way of saying "Oneness," isn't that an experience of being joined with All?

If we are lucky enough to have an experience in which we become aware of the Oneness that surrounds us, even for a brief time, it's extremely helpful in keeping us in touch with the possibility of finding relief from relentless ego thoughts. The memory provides us with a gentle reminder of our goal—that of achieving lasting peace and stillness.

My Worth is Intrinsic

"The logic of worldly success rests on a fallacy: the
strange error that our perfection depends on the thoughts
and opinions and applause of other men!" ~ THOMAS MERTON

Each of us is part of Oneness, and thus it follows that each of us has intrinsic worth. In other words, our worth is established by God—not by our education, work ethic, status, or wealth. Accepting the mere possibility of this premise being true is absolutely essential to our mental health and happiness. It is also crucial to the successful processing of powerfully negative beliefs. We simply cannot be flawed, less than, or bad if our worth is intrinsic, unchangeable, and non-negotiable. This concept leaves no room for self-imposed guilt, shame and self-doubt, and provides a rock-solid concept of self.

The person who holds the record for the shortest stay at the El Cielo Center is an accountant with a busy international practice, whose stress level was extremely high when he arrived. His takeaway after only two sessions was: "My worth is intrinsic." That understanding allowed him to achieve even greater levels of success in his career in a relaxed and easy way. Previously he had been driven by a deeply held belief in his unworthiness. This belief had pushed him to amplified levels of apparent success in order to hide the "truth" of who he was from himself and everyone else. He had felt himself to be a fraud all of his life.

Does this sound familiar?

After absorbing this idea, his clear understanding that he had no need to prove himself to anyone gave him tremendous freedom to transform his work life, from being characterized by exhausted frustration to enjoyment, in which he could freely give and receive. All the energy that had previously gone into striving was now freed up and transformed into truly creative energy.

The Truth is that our worth is established by God. No one and nothing can ever change that, no matter who we think we are, no matter what we do or don't do. It is this Eternal Self that we return to when we do this work. The Six-Step Process will help you completely transform your being by reconnecting to that Truth of who you really are. In so doing, you shift gradually and lovingly from an ego-based, fear-based existence, to being heart-centered and love-based—your true Self. You are able to understand, from a place of deep confidence, that whatever is happening *to* you is happening *for* you. Your perception of all challenges and difficulties will thus be transformed.

I compare my real Self to a loving GPS which tells me, "At

the next turn, make a right." If I don't make a right, 'Self' doesn't then say—as the ego would—"You stupid jerk, I told you to make a right! Now you're on your own!" Instead, it recalculates the route ahead and repeats, "At the next turn make a right." No matter how long I ignore it, the loving GPS of Self will recalculate and tell me the next best move to make—which might include a U-turn.

Of the people who come to our center, probably 99 percent are not even aware that they have a spiritual GPS. They're completely and totally reliant on that other, more dominant guidance system: the ego. The ego is a belief system based on the idea that something is wrong with you. The ego is the belief that you're bad, not lovable, depressed and deprived, and separate from everything around you. All these ideas are false directions to follow, but I sure did for fifty years.

> *"There is no such thing as a person. There are only restrictions and limitations. The sum total of these defines the person. The person merely appears to be, like the space within the pot appears to have the shape and volume and smell of the pot."* ~ NISARGADATTA

Separation of the Ego

Now that we have looked at who we are in Truth, let's focus on why we feel separate from others and from Oneness. We must have done something terribly wrong to be excluded, to be kicked out of God's club, as it were. The horrible thing is, we don't have a clue about what we did wrong—and yet we all walk around with a chronic, low-grade sense of guilt. When this low-grade feeling of gnawing guilt gets to be so all pervasive it affects our work, our sleep, and our relationships, we might visit a doctor or a psychiatrist, whereupon that condition is diagnosed by any number of labels and we are offered medication.

The archetypal myth of Adam and Eve in the Garden of Eden, eating the forbidden fruit, can be interpreted as a parable about mankind's split from God, or Oneness. Prior to eating the fruit, Adam and Eve existed blissfully as part of Oneness. The "bad apple" grew not just on any apple tree but on the "Tree of Knowledge." With that one bite, we lost Knowing Oneness, and started pursuing the world's kind of knowledge. We began naming and classifying and establishing the differences of everything, especially the difference of self and "other."

Can you imagine what your world would look like if you did not 'see' other? By seeing other I mean experiencing separation at a variety of levels. With that bite of the apple also came sexual shame, a fundamental experience of "other," symbolized by a fig leaf.

Each of us develops and nourishes our own specific 'reasons' for feeling guilty, but underlying it all is the sense that we no longer feel connected to God at the primal level. In my case, guilt associated with my mother and the camps provided me with plenty of early evidence of my wrongness.

Loss and suffering, mourning, sadness, and anger, all the feelings that seem to make up the human condition, derive from the fundamental belief "I am separate." But where do these thoughts and feelings come from—these thoughts that separate us from Oneness? We choose them based on who we think we are—but again, who we think we are is not who we really are in Truth.

The Truth of Our Innocence

While the common denominator of the ego-self that we all make up is guilt, the common denominator of our true Self is

innocence. When I introduce this concept at workshops, people are shocked. It is a wildly radical idea, this unchangeable
innocence. And it brings up a fascinating array of confessions:

- "How can I possibly be innocent? I stole money from my
  partner to buy my next hit of cocaine. This man trusted
  me with our company account. I'm guilty!"
- "I cheated on my husband, how could I possibly be
  innocent?"
- "If you knew how I make a living, you would know how
  ridiculous that idea of 'innocence' is."

Let me explain: We can't be guilty in Truth, because we are
an integral part of Oneness. Since we think we are on this little
planet and clearly no longer part of this mystical Oneness, we
must have done something to be kicked out. Whatever it is, we
think we did something wrong. To sustain that belief, we have to
attract evidence or the belief withers. So we will set out to prove
the validity of our belief in guilt by stealing money, procra-
stinating, cheating, lying, or any other form our belief in guilt
might choose to take.

The "I" who tries to get others to agree that guilt is real is an
"I" that we made up—a set of beliefs that could never be True.
It has nothing to do with the unchangeable Self we are. Who we
are in Truth is not affected at all by our perceived guilt, nor by
our 'guilty' behavior.

Someone who has fully integrated this teaching would not
react emotionally to having money stolen, being called names, or
being betrayed or cheated on. This person might have an initial
reaction or upset, but it would soon be welcomed as a healing
opportunity and processed. Peace would quickly be regained.

The more committed we are to knowing who we truly are, the shorter an upset is likely to last. That is because a trained individual is committed to seeing the innocence of self and others at all times. She is committed to seeing the Truth of each of us, and not to believe the guilty story we bring to the table. She can see our innocence, and know that our behavior is merely a reflection of who we think we are.

I call this "holding the space" and it is the key to success in a healing relationship. Many years ago, our healing center was not set up the way it is now and security was not foremost on our minds. One morning a staff member knocked on my bedroom door to report that we had been robbed—and not just robbed, for the entire safe had been pried off its concrete base and removed. My response? "Oh, well." (I actually don't remember saying that, but the staff member repeated it often as an example how an upset is not an upset till we decide it is.)

If I refuse to buy into your story, if I am not seeing you as your behavior, if I refuse to allow that who you are is a changeable, small, weak, victim, ego self, then I will not reflect your guilt back to you and you will have the space required to come back to who you are in Truth. If I remember the Truth of you, then in that reflection you are helped to recognize the Truth of yourself. If you see me not reacting, not even being affected by your story or behavior, you will be reminded of your own innocence. Then you have an opportunity to stop pursuing evidence for old mistaken beliefs.

A business partner whose company funds were misused to support a cocaine habit may well be upset that his money has been stolen—but this upset has nothing to do with what happened. The upset was chosen by an old belief that the world is not safe, that he is not loved, or that he's doomed to be a victim. What is so fascinating is that when we get to work on processing upsets like these, we invariably find that somehow, at an unconscious level, the partner actually chose the cocaine user as a partner in order to collect evidence for his own beliefs. There were early warning signs. They are in this dance together.

Similarly, a husband whose wife cheats on him may have subconsciously chosen that wife in order to replay an ancient hurt and deliver evidence for his beliefs that he is unlovable, a victim, or that he can be abandoned.

You can see why I am so inspired to work with an entire family. Members of a family can start to see the patterns of family behavior, as well as the roles they play within that system. Beliefs run in the family, as it were. And the whole family needs to heal their beliefs if they want to be loving and functional. Often, the parent of a child with substance abuse issues will help that child enormously just by working on themselves. Achieving acceptance of their own innocence can be the key to healing their child's addictions. When the child ceases to be evidence for the parents' beliefs that they are bad, not good enough, or guilty, then the child is free to start healing his own mistaken beliefs. It is almost as if the parent has made a deal with his child: "I need you to be an addict (or drop out of school, or hang out with the wrong crowd) so I get to be right that I am a bad father!" Insane? Of course, and yet all parents play this out at some level. The bottom line is that guilt in Truth is not an option.

That said, seeing the innocence of an abusive parent can be difficult.

A 42-year-old with terminal cancers of the ovaries, uterus, and pelvis came to see me. What came out in the course of our time together was that she had been sexually abused by her father, brother, and uncles. Virtually every male in her life had abused her, with her father having been the main culprit. Not surprisingly, she was absolutely consumed with hatred for all of these men, her father in particular.

After listening lovingly to her story, I began to introduce to her the teachings we've discussed above. Yes, awful things had happened, but they had happened to her body. Her suffering was a direct result how what had happened had been interpreted by her and society. Awful things did happen to her body and as long as she only saw herself as a body, her suffering would go on unabated. There is no problem imaginable, no suffering possible that does not have its roots in body identification. She was not yet prepared to allow her anger to ease just a little, so that she might see that there was another way to reflect on her horrendous past. By the third session, when I realized that she was not prepared to shift her interpretation of the past; I tried another tack. I said to her, "Can you say, 'My father's innocent and I love him"?

She exploded, replying "Haven't you heard a word I've said? That bastard should rot in jail and I will do whatever I can to make sure that happens!"

To this I answered, "I did hear that." And then I restated the question: "Can you say, 'My father's innocent and I love him'?" Same violent reaction. Then I asked: "What would it cost you to say, 'My father's innocent'?"

Without missing a beat, she replied, "It would cost me myself."

Precisely! The victim self she had made up was the only self she knew. She wasn't ready to relinquish that identity. She had spent years going to incest victim support groups where her unhappy identity was not only welcomed and justified, but actively reinforced. She was not willing at that point to allow the reality that she had a capital "S" Self, abiding and eternal, which nothing could harm and which was not affected by any of the events of her life. She was addicted to being a victim, and habituated to the anger, depression, and hopelessness that came from that identity.

You might say: "She had every reason to be angry; furious in fact." That would be right. However, our work utilizes a simple question that the ego hates: "Do I want to be right —that all the evidence of my stories corroborates that I am indeed a victim— or do I want to be happy knowing that my True Self cannot be a victim?" That is the one question I ask myself every time I'm tempted to see myself as unfairly treated, not supported, or betrayed. Clearly "being right" can give the illusion of happiness, an illusion of superiority or strength, but that doesn't last.

To begin healing we must be willing to say: "I must be wrong because I am not happy." With this realization we have made a real start at reversing cause and effect. The cause is within and the effect is seen as outside.

Remembering who we are

The True Self is Oneness, God, Love; it is all we are. Ego is the thought that we are always alone, the thought that we are not attractive, the thought that we will always be alone.... one thought like this after another. The ego is only a thought, a thought of separation. Therefore it doesn't exist because in essence, there's no such thing as separation. However, if we don't learn that there's no such thing as separation, then the only voice we will ever hear is the voice of the ego. We will never hear another voice, because the voice of the loving Self does not overrule the ego; it doesn't even argue with it.

It just waits. It waits for us to say, "The crap my ego feeds me day in and day out doesn't work for me anymore. There has to be another way."

In order to remember who I am and always have been, I use a radical form of forgiveness. But the forgiveness I am referring to has nothing to do with what anyone may have done to me or what I may have done to anyone else. The forgiveness I practice has to do with transforming my core beliefs about myself and who I am in the world. It's about rethinking and then rectifying the idea that I could be separate from the rest of existence; the idea that I could be hurt; the idea that I could be alone; the idea that I could be vulnerable; the idea that I could be merely a body; and, most of all, the idea that I could be guilty.

Not one of these ideas has any truth in it. In Truth you and I are one with all of Creation at all times, in fact, outside of time. We are not separate or alone, and when we apply the transformative power of forgiveness, we forgive ourselves for believing in separation. Who we are in Truth is unchanged and unchangeable, who we are in Truth is eternal and infinite.

Given that love is the essence of our True being, it follows that loving thoughts come from our true Self. Fear-based thoughts come from the ego. Once we recognize this, we are able to monitor our thoughts and intercept the ones that don't serve us. Little by little, we will transform our life experience by training the mind. The Six Steps to Freedom, described in the remaining pages of this book, provide a useful tool for this endeavor. The rewards for using it will be beyond anything you can now imagine.

And, please be aware that this radical transformation process will at times feel like your entire world is being turned upside down. That is because it is.

*"Imagine yourself as a living house. God comes in to rebuild
that house. At first, perhaps, you can understand what He is
doing. He is getting the drains right and stopping the leaks in the
roof and so on; you knew that those jobs needed doing and so you are
not surprised. But presently He starts knocking the house about
in a way that hurts abominably and does not seem to make any
sense. What on earth is He up to? The explanation is that He is
building quite a different house from the one you thought of—
throwing out a new wing here, putting on an extra floor there,
running up towers, making courtyards. You thought you
were being made into a decent little cottage: but He
is building a palace. He intends to come
and live in it Himself."* ~ C.S. LEWIS

SUMMARY

1) Oneness is our True reality.
2) An experience of Oneness is helpful in remembering who we are in Truth.
3) Our worth is intrinsic.
4) We are innocent in Truth.
5) Our unhappiness stems from the belief that we are separate.
6) We can shift our attention from our ego 'self' to our 'Self' by training our mind and in so doing regain happiness, which is our birthright.
7) Love is all there is.

CHAPTER 4

The 'Choose Again' Six-Step Process
To Emotional Freedom

"Projection makes perception. The world you see is
what you gave it, nothing more than that. But though it is
no more than that, it is not less. Therefore, to you it is important.
It is the witness to your state of mind, the outside picture of an inward
condition. As a man thinketh, so does he perceive. Therefore, seek not
to change the world, but choose to change your mind about the
world. Perception is a result and not a cause."
~ A COURSE IN MIRACLES

O N THE following pages we will explore a simple process
that I use to find emotional freedom from any conflict or
upset that I have in my life. I've introduced this process to
thousands of people, and they too have found it an effective way
to work with their thoughts and emotions—to transform their
daily state of mind from one of turmoil to one of inner peace
and happiness. You will find it to be a relationship saver and
a virtually foolproof conflict resolution tool. If you practice this
process just a few times each day, you are bound to change your
life in ways you cannot yet imagine.

This Six-Step Process is simple, yet radical and transformative. When utilizing it, I focus on an everyday upset, big or small,
and examine that upset in order to uncover a core belief I have
about myself. Knowing how erroneous that belief is, I forgive

myself for holding it, and remind myself that, given the truth of who I really am, that belief could never be true. The small self that my ego has constructed—which is really nothing more than a cluster of beliefs—is what I am setting out to transform when I undertake this work.

The set of beliefs I've made up goes by the name "Diederik." Beliefs and their expressions are really what society calls "character" or "personality". You and I are not lazy, or attractive, dishonest or argumentative... we just believe we are. And how we behave when these beliefs go unquestioned serves to confirm and reinforce our beliefs about ourselves. By correcting my beliefs using the Six-Step Process—and thereby literally changing my mind—I actually alter deeply entrenched patterns of behavior that are sabotaging my ability to experience an emotionally healthy, harmonious and happy life.

The Six-Step Process begins with any upset, and ends with profound healing. Ordinary everyday upsets become the portals to happiness. For example, if someone cuts me off in traffic, a classic upset for so many of us, I can apply the Six-Step Process to that upset. After discovering which embedded belief chose my emotional response to that event, I can correct it. Perhaps it's my belief that I'm a victim. If so, I use the Six Steps to process that belief. Whichever belief has been triggered, that's what I examine and transform.

After I've successfully completed the process, I'll be able to encounter a similar situation without the need to honk the horn, yell colorful language out the window, or make angry gestures at the offending driver. Being cut off in traffic becomes a neutral event that doesn't hold any emotion for me, if I've done the work to correct the beliefs that drove (no pun intended) my behavior. So you see how an upset contains the gift of a forgiveness opportunity!

"...feelings like disappointment, embarrassment, irritation, resentment, anger, jealousy, and fear, instead of being bad news, are actually very clear moments that teach us where it is that we're holding back. They teach us to perk up and lean in when we feel we'd rather collapse and back away. They're like messengers that show us, with terrifying clarity, exactly where we're stuck. This very moment is the perfect teacher, and, lucky for us, it's with us wherever we are."
~ PEMA CHODRON

Everything in my life is the result of my thoughts, and my thoughts are unconsciously directed by my beliefs.

One teaching from *A Course in Miracles* that invariably incurs immediate and intense resistance is: "It is my thoughts alone that cause me pain." The resistance is chosen by a powerful belief, the belief in being a victim. At the moment the planet is populated by some seven billion people, most of them convinced they are victims. Victims of their parents, their children, their boss, the weather, the economy... you get the idea? We are addicted to the feelings of victimization.

What the Six-Step Process will teach you, amongst several other crucial new insights, is that you are the absolute author of your experience on the planet. Victims can roll their eyes now: "I did not choose to lose my father when I was just four years old." That may be true, but it's also true that the meaning you gave it was your choice. I am never upset at a fact, but at my interpretation of that fact.

As Marcus Aurelius said a long time ago: "If you are distressed by anything external, the pain is not due to the thing itself, but to your estimate of it; and this you have the power to revoke at any moment." Shakespeare said much the same in Hamlet: "There is nothing either good or bad, but thinking makes it so."How many of us are immediately prepared to accept this truth without the slightest objection: "Yeah, but...?" It took me awhile but I discovered fairly early in my process that the problems and challenges I faced became much less daunting once I accepted true responsibility, and moved out of the realm of victimhood.

All aspects of my existence are nothing more than pieces of evidence that support core beliefs. So, that means that if I want a different outcome—literally, a different reality—I must change my mind. I must change my mind about who I think I am. Here are the steps to do that.

Step One: **Recognize That "I Am Upset"**

Every day we all face numerous incidents that upset us in one way or another. For the purpose of healing my mistaken beliefs, any feeling I experience that is not peaceful is considered to be an upset. In order to begin healing, I have to start paying attention to each and every one of these upsets. The first thing I must do when I get upset is to acknowledge that I am upset or in conflict. In so doing I must fully own the upset. When I am not at peace I am upset; you can't be both at once. And that means there is no such thing as a small upset—in the same sense that you can't be a little bit pregnant.

Every upset presents an opportunity for me to find and dismantle one of the barriers I have to inner peace. That's exciting! Now I can welcome upsets as catalysts for my healing. When I'm upset I've been given a golden opportunity to feel the feeling and allow the feeling to guide me back to the source. The upset is triggering a memory of an earlier time when I felt the same way, that's all. It is an echo of an event that was over long ago.

We'll develop this idea further in the following chapter, but for now, just hold that thought and trust that it's true. All upsets or emotional disturbances serve the same purpose: to prove that my mistaken beliefs about myself are true.

STEP TWO: **Me, It's About Me**

*"Why is everyone here so happy except me?" a disciple asked.
"Because they have learned to see goodness and beauty everywhere,"
said the Master. "Why don't I see goodness and beauty everywhere?"
"Because you cannot see outside of you what you fail to see inside."*
~ ANTHONY DE MELLO, SJ

There is a powerful teaching from *A Course in Miracles* that says: **I am never upset for the reason I think**. Step Two teaches me that whenever I'm upset or in conflict, it's never about another person or an external situation. It is never about what I think it is about, however much I want to be right when I am upset. Instead, it's just about me. But my old voice will counter that: "Yeah right," it protests, "this time it really IS someone else's fault, not mine—and here's why!" Then the 'why' becomes the immediate justification for the upset. If I run with the justification I'll miss the gift: healing the belief that chose the upset.

With Step Two, all that finger-pointing must go. It is much easier to adopt the role of a victim than it is to take complete and total responsibility for my experience in life. When I accept that I'm the author of my own life, and the author of each and every circumstance of my life, I have to let go of blame. I have to let go of all blame. Blaming others and/or blaming myself only serves to strengthen a negative belief that I have about myself. I have to let go of the story. In the story I am right. In the story I have every reason to be upset, and even worse, I am justified in being traumatized for life, damaged beyond repair. That means I have become my story, and to that degree my upsets are justified.

"When you plant lettuce, if it does not grow well, you don't blame the lettuce. You look for reasons it is not doing well. It may need fertilizer, or more water, or less sun. You never blame the lettuce. Yet if we have problems with our friends or family, we blame the other person. But if we know how to take care of them, they will grow well, like the lettuce. Blaming has no positive effect at all, nor does trying to persuade using reason and argument. That is my experience. No blame, no reasoning, no argument, just understanding. If you understand, and you show that you understand, you can love, and the situation will change."
~ Thich Nhat Hanh

Step Two is a powerful anti-victim step, where healing begins. I must learn to take responsibility for everything in my life—which is essentially an empowering process—without assigning blame. I now know that blaming someone else for the conflict will not get me what I really want, and that is to be happy, to be at peace. Step Two is the most important and most difficult step of them all; we will look at this in much greater detail in Chapter Six.

Step Three: **Feel My Feelings**

Now I ask myself "What am I feeling?" It's surprising, how hard it sometimes is to know what I'm really feeling. This is where commitment to honesty is essential. As mentioned earlier, when I started on my own healing path, I had only two distinct feelings: numbness and rage. Numbness was the big one, although I did get perverse pleasure—an illusory sense of being powerful—from a chronic state of rage. In Step Three, I have to take the time to identify my dominant feeling, or my two or three strongest feelings, and allow myself to experience them completely by feeling at a very deep level.

I must become deeply familiar with my feelings because I have to be "in the feeling" in order to make a genuine change in my life. That is, I have to feel it to heal it. Why? Because it's the feelings that will lead me to a memory or memories of situations in which I felt this way before (coming up in Step 4). Those memories allow me to access an understanding of the root cause of the development of each core belief I have—access to who I think I am.

Remember, hiding beneath each feeling is an emotion-charged memory that forms the foundation of an erroneous belief about myself. All this happened at a very early age. So in order to unpack each feeling that I'm currently experiencing, I have to focus on it—make it as big a feeling as I possibly can—and really, really feel it.

Because, again, if I don't feel it, I can't heal it.

Step Four: **Remember When I First Felt This Way**

Now that I am "in the feeling" I ask myself: "Is this feeling familiar? Have there been other circumstances where I also felt like this?" It is impossible that this is the first time I have felt this way, because emotional reactions are actually just replays of events from a long time ago. This awareness helps me to accept that the feeling I have chosen has nothing to do with the current circumstance of the upset. The circumstance simply "triggered" or activated a feeling that is chosen by a core belief.

Once I realize that my feelings manifest in patterns, I have to become a detective. I am looking for the source of this feeling so I ask myself: "When did I first feel this way?" After a little searching the feeling will trigger a memory, I'll remember an old incident when someone said or did something that made me feel that same way. I may have to go back pretty far in my memory to find the first instance of a particular feeling, but find it I will.

When I do find the memory, I need to ask myself: "On a scale of 1 to 10, how strong is this feeling within the memory?" A 10 would mean that I am so upset I can hardly stand it, whereas a 1 would be minimal emotion.

Step Five: Establish My Mistaken Judgment of Myself

So here I am, in the middle of my process: I'm clearly upset, I've taken ownership of it, and it's bringing up all my "stuff." I am determined to do my work, so I stay in the feeling and allow the early memory of an upset to play out in my mind like a replay in sports. Now my job is to focus on the memory that's arisen and ask myself: Who am I in this situation? How did I interpret the situation or circumstance in which this feeling played such a strong role?

Also, if there were other people involved in that early circumstance, I might ask myself: How do I think that other person judged me when he spoke to me that way? And—most importantly—what was my judgment of myself in that defining moment? What did it say about me that that person acted or spoke that way? What kind of person deserves to be treated this way? What kind of person deserves to feel this way?

To give an example from my life: My father was a drinker and his behavior could be very unpredictable. On occasion, as I was growing up, he would be very angry at me for no discernible reason. This happened frequently. As I reached back in my mind to examine the very first memory of this kind, I found that I had blamed myself for his anger. I judged myself as guilty. There must have been something wrong with me to provoke such an unexpected response from him. Ever after that, when someone was angry at me for no apparent reason, my default program would be to blame myself. In years of working with people it has become so clear that having a parent with a substance abuse issue leaves one constantly on edge, constantly waiting for the 'other shoe to drop.'

As you can see, this interpretation of a childhood event led me to establish a mistaken belief about myself, one that I carried with me as part of my core identity for a good part of my life. Step Six is the way to undo that, and any other belief.

Step Six: **Embrace the Truth About Me**

In this final step you correct the negative self-judgment that you identified in Step Five, with a two-part forgiveness process. First you shift your perceptions about that childhood circumstance, and what you mistakenly thought it said about you. The belief you formed about who you were at that point was wrong, and never served you. The second part of forgiveness is to remember that who you are in Truth — Love itself — is unchanged and unchangeable.

Let's go back to the example of my father drinking, and how I misused that fact to judge myself as guilty. Now is the time to undo that belief. So I say to myself: "Forgive me for believing that I am guilty. Thank God that is not true, I just made it up. It is just an erroneous belief that I can now let go of." I go on to ask myself for forgiveness for every belief I made up at the time (weak, powerless, unworthy, unimportant, shameful, undeserving of love, not good enough, didn't belong, a victim etc.). In my experience most of us have one or more of these limiting beliefs.

I may have to do this forgiveness exercise more than once;

old beliefs are sometimes hard to shake. After all, I am now changing my entire identity! I am setting out to change the idea of myself that I have lived with for many years.

The second part of this forgiveness process is to confirm the Truth of me. This time I forgive myself for forgetting the Truth of who I am. I may say, for example:

- "Forgive me for forgetting that who I am is unchangeably innocent."
- "Forgive me for forgetting that my worth is intrinsic, and is not established by what I do or think."
- "Forgive me for forgetting that I am an integral and unchangeable part of the Oneness of Love."

My response (to myself) is: "Thank God that is the Truth."

It is important to correct each belief I uncovered in the upset. So if I believed that I was powerless, I will now remember that I am the author of my own experience, and that my power (the power of Love) is infinite.

Where am I at now?

Time to check in with the level of my feelings, so I go back into the memory I conjured up in Step Four. How do I feel now? Chances are that I have much less of an emotional reaction to the circumstances in my memory. My goal is to be at peace. If I am not fully at peace I need to repeat the process, and look at other negative beliefs, until the upset is completely neutralized. Rarely it happens that the upset has not been reduced in intensity, does not feel better, or perhaps even worse. In this case it is likely that there is an earlier or different origin for the upset, which can be found by repeating all the steps.

Forgiveness is what I use in this process. However, it is

important to note that I'm not forgiving my father for drinking, or my teachers for getting angry and yelling at me.

I want to be very clear: this kind of forgiveness is not about condoning anyone's unacceptable behavior. Rather, I am forgiving myself for the beliefs I made up, as a result of the early circumstances in question. I am forgiving myself for believing that I am what I never could be: worthless or unlovable, or powerless, or guilty.

This process sets me free. When I practice it frequently, it radically changes all my relationships. That is because all of my relationships are with my 'self' and I am now transforming that little 's' self to connect with my big 'S' eternal, universal, Self.

SUMMARY

Challenge yourself to remember each step of the Choose Again Six-Step Process using the "I'M FREE" mnemonic. Teach the process to a friend — that's the best way to secure the knowledge!

Here's the mnemonic shorthand of the Six-Step Process:

STEP 1: **I**'m upset

STEP 2: **M**e: It's about me

STEP 3: **F**ocus on the feelings

STEP 4: **R**emember my ancient feelings

STEP 5: **E**stablish my judgment of myself

STEP 6: **E**mbrace the truth about me

(Note that the first letters of the steps spells out I'M FREE.)

Chapter 5

Step One:
Recognize That "I am Upset"

*"I get irritated, I get upset. Especially when I'm in a hurry.
But I see it all as part of our training. To get irritated is
to lose our way in life."* ~ Haruki Murakami

C HECK TO see if any of these complaints rings a bell:
"She always criticizes me in public."
"My son is out so late and I'm worried!"
"I just don't fit in here."
"Where did she put the remote?"
"I wish he would not do it that way."
"That man has 14 items, what is he doing in the express lane?"

From the time we wake up in the morning till we go to bed at night, we are presented with countless opportunities to get upset. Sadly, we rarely pass up any of these offerings. For the purpose of this chapter, we'll define an upset as any state of mind other than peaceful or happy. So, being worried, sad, angry, bored, annoyed, anxious, depressed, lonely or even slightly irritated is an "upset."

The good news is that upsets are gold if we learn to see them that way. Now what do I mean by "an upset is gold"? It's simply this: every upset serves a purpose. Actually every upset serves two diametrically opposing purposes. From the ego's point of view, the purpose is to prove that my beliefs are correct—in other words, an upset serves as evidence of what I believe. From my higher Self's point of view, the upset gives me an opportunity to realize that a mistaken core belief has chosen evidence to provoke an upset—and that now I can correct the belief. This can be hard to accept sometimes.

Let's break this down a little. How many of us are used to being mildly upset, irritated, disappointed, or just out-of-sorts many times every day? I know I am. How did I use to deal with these disturbances? I would push them aside, ignore them. It's not a big deal, I'd say to myself. Or: Don't sweat the small stuff. Or I'd pour a glass of decent wine or smoke a joint. One thing is for sure: I would blame myself, someone or something, since there had to be a cause "out there" for my upset. I had a whole range of such coping techniques, but in the long run they didn't work. In the long run, in fact, not only do coping techniques fail, they may lead to depression, chronic anxiety, and even physical illness.

To be really happy, we must become increasingly vigilant about noting and then processing as many upsets as we possibly can each and every day. "That sounds like hard work," you say. Well, yes, but would you agree that it may be a whole lot easier than being miserably unhappy—or even slightly annoyed—most of your life? Over time, it provides a much higher payoff than downing three martinis a day at lunchtime, or filing for that second divorce.

The following is an example of someone who had been doing this work for a while, but got tripped up one day after receiving an e-mail that upset him. Here's Taylor's account of this incident:

"Some days it feels like it doesn't take much to upset me. The difference, after becoming aware of my thoughts and feelings, is that I can now interrupt my thoughts and resulting behaviors by noticing that I'm upset. I'll give you an example.

"At the time, I was looking for a new job—something that, like most people, I've always found quite stressful. One day I was following up on a promising lead with the hiring manager at a company I thought I'd enjoy working for, and I received a short e-mail response from him after submitting my resume.

"My immediate thought upon receiving this curt reply was that I wasn't qualified for the position. My interpretation was that he didn't think I was capable of handling the job, given my experience. This conclusion put me into a tailspin, and pretty soon I was thinking that I would never find a new job. Physically, I felt my heart rate increase. In my car on the way to a meeting, I was so distracted that I wasn't paying any attention to my driving. I wasn't very present or aware of my surroundings on the road!

"Noticing and then acknowledging this, I pulled over for a few minutes in order to process my upset. Being aware of my thoughts and feelings allowed me to change my mind. A few short minutes later, I had a clear head and was ready to engage in my meeting in a fully present state.

"The funny thing is, when I really stopped to think about it, nothing had actually happened. I read an e-mail, assigned a certain meaning to it, and started beating myself up mentally because of my interpretation of it. After processing the upset I could see the communication for what it actually was—a completely neutral acknowledgment of the resume that I had sent—nothing more, and nothing less."

As you can see from this example, Taylor was completely honest with himself about what was going on, which allowed him to fully and quickly process the incident, and regain peace. It is important to note that if he completed the Six-Step Process and truly healed the triggered belief, then he would not only get over this incident, but similar upsets in the future would be reduced since that belief would no longer be in play, or at least its power is diminished. This underscores the need we all have to be aware, at all times, of our emotional state.

"Everyone creates realities based on their own personal beliefs. These beliefs are so powerful that they can create expansive or entrapping realities over and over." ~ KUAN YIN

A big part of this first step is to not accept the ego's first explanation or justification for any upset. Instead, we need to learn that we are never upset for the reason we think. So, take a deep breath and repeat to yourself: "I am never upset for the reason I think." Any upset triggers feelings within us that are derived from our reaction to something that happened in our past. You may find it a challenge, but it's important to resist the temptation to say: "I'm upset because…" The 'because' is the justification that your belief is choosing in order not to heal. Sounds a bit perverse, does it not? Yes, but it is a perversity of your own making. Here is an example of this from my own life.

Many years ago a group of dedicated practitioners and I

founded an organization dedicated to working with youth-at-risk. One of the co-leaders of that organization, a powerful presence, indicated that she might leave the group. I had a huge emotional response which was out of proportion to the circumstances of the situation.

I knew that a quick process would bring me to a calm and rational understanding of the situation. So I went back to the feeling of intense fear and deep loss that the woman's words had brought up in me—and I allowed the feeling to balloon to the point where I was literally heaving with emotion.

And then it came back to me. The feeling went back to the camps and the time my brother had taken me with him to forage for edible leaves. We had to sneak under the fence to the 'outside' in order to find the plant material. This was a risky endeavour for, if caught, we would be severely punished. My brother was older than me, and he was the leader. I trusted him like no other, for my life was quite literally in his hands. One wrong move by him and we would both be in peril.

Cut to my colleague announcing that she might be leaving and my seemingly disproportionate feeling response. I quickly realized that I had transferred that ancient trust in my brother to her and, at some deep unconscious level, made her into the one person in our organization whom I could trust with my life—not only that, but I needed her for my very survival.

I processed that and have not had an analogous reaction since then. (And she did not leave, I'm happy to report.)

There are no small upsets

In addition to understanding that I'm never upset for the reason I think, it's also important to remember that there are no small upsets. All of them are equally disturbing to my peace of mind. If I truly wish to be at peace, I must be vigilant and catch even the smallest irritation. I must acknowledge that I have been triggered somehow, take ownership of my experience, and be determined to get to the root of it.

Here's an example: One day at our center in Costa Rica Patty's husband Simon had offered to make a chocolate cake for the whole group at the center to enjoy. This triggered a reaction in Patty, which she explained as follows: she was upset 'because' Simon was always making chocolate cakes to impress their guests. As I just said: beware of the 'because'! Even though Patty typically did most of the cooking for their frequent visitors, Simon would be the one to get the attention and the accolades for his cakes or other baked goods.

In circle, Patty agreed to process her reaction and she recalled an event wherein she had baked a chocolate cake for a contest held by her Girl Guide troop. Patty didn't win, despite being absolutely convinced that nothing could beat her grandmother's chocolate cake recipe. Her best friend's Florentine's entry was really better by far, but Patty couldn't accept that at the time, and behaved very badly in protesting the judges' outcome.

Her anger and sense of being unfairly treated was so strong that Patty and her best friend had an irreparable falling out. Then, Patty blamed herself for being "bad," "a heinous creature," and even "unworthy of love." These major beliefs were sorely in need of correction, which Patty proceeded to do in circle. As a seemingly trivial upset was resolved, the end result was a significant healing for Patty.

Thus any upset, however small it seems, may lead to great progress in the shifting of old and stubborn beliefs. Patty's initial reaction to her husband making the cake was: "He is going to get love for this, which means there is less love for me." The belief behind it: "Love comes from outside of me, I do not have any myself." To Patty, validation and recognition by others was a substitute for loving the Self. By correcting these erroneous beliefs she cleared the barriers to love—the beliefs that stood in the way of her knowing who she really is, which is Love itself.

What is it for?

All day long we need to check in with this question: "How am I feeling?" The answer might be: "I'm upset. I'm either angry, sad, or whatever it is, but I'm upset. There's something going on, I am believing something, I'm not at peace." That's the first step.

If something indeed appears to be very "wrong" then someone trained in applying the Six-Step process to all upsets will almost immediately ask, "What is this for?" That means one is willing to look for the healing opportunity inherent in the upset. A person trained in the Six-Step Process will not ask: "Why did this happen?" because that question implies that someone did something wrong. "What is it for?" implies that the incident contains a gift, although we may not be seeing that gift right at that moment. It's our job to figure out what the gift is.

Eventually, we'll be able to see that nothing ever goes "wrong." In the beginning, that recognition may require a leap of faith. Learning to make that leap will deliver surprising dividends.

I am very aware that taking the faith-based position that nothing ever goes wrong is a huge stretch, and may even seem offensive to some. Just be with it for awhile, and you'll see how your perception of the world starts shifting.

At a recent workshop we enjoyed the presence of a most vociferous participant. In the first few days of the weeklong event she allowed us many glimpses into the fearful, angry, suspicious world she had made up for herself. Much of her anger and fear was directed at the fact that 'immigrants were moving into the neighborhood.' One story featured a black cab driver, who had turned on his GPS in order to drive her to the airport, which she somehow found personally insulting. Why? Because she felt that using a GPS was symptomatic of incompetence, of not being trustworthy, of being an unwanted foreigner, and so on. As she ranted about all this, all of us in the healing circle maintained our focus, just listening. If one listens carefully, the person sharing a story will inevitably tell you exactly who they think they are.

When she wound down, I asked her if there could be, perhaps, another way of interpreting the cab driver story. There was not, she was adamant. So I asked everyone if there might be another way of seeing this event, another interpretation. One by one the alternative interpretations started to flow:

- "He was a new driver and wanted to make sure he chose the quickest route."
- "He was simply following company policy."
- "He had heard there was some construction along the planned route and he wanted to make sure to avoid it."
- "He had a rough night and was not too sure about how to get there."
- "A previous passenger had accused him of taking an unnecessary long way."
- "By checking his GPS device, he could provide a number of possible routes that the client could choose from."
- "The driver was providing transparency in his operations so that the client could know exactly where he was going."

All in all, about fifteen different ways of seeing the situation were presented, and none of them would have led to an upset. Remember, we are never upset at a fact, only at our interpretation of that fact. Every experience I have on this planet is the result of my interpretation. That interpretation is chosen by the self I made up, the set of beliefs I call 'me.'

The woman listened, although she kept wanting to interrupt, but was repeatedly encouraged to take in the information being offered. She remained resistant to any other way of seeing that day, but the next morning she spoke up first in the group to say: "I have thought about it and realized it's possible that the cab driver was trying to be helpful." This was a major breakthrough: this woman had never allowed anyone to help her, and thus to allow the idea of being helped was incredibly healing. It confronted a core belief at the center of her ego, and was therefore hard to accept at first.

If we only suffer from our interpretation of an event, then the event itself is not important. Sit with that for a moment. You might well ask: "Are you saying that the trauma of incest is the same as a stubbed toe?" Now, that sounds absolutely insane. And yet, yes, ultimately that is what I teach. The "I" whom I've made up is choosing my experience of any event. Whatever happens to your body in no way alters who you truly are, and has no effect on the love at the core of your being. Whether you stub a toe, break an arm, or suffer molestation, all these traumas happen to the body. The issue is body identification: the thought that we are our bodies.

For many years we have worked with a considerable number of clients who suffered sexual, physical, or emotional abuse. It may come as a surprise to you that as soon as a client recognizes the profound validity of what we teach, they begin to heal—

"Yes, someone did something to your body, we do not ever question that. But what you have done with it, how you have interpreted the event that is your responsibility." With this perspective, they no longer see themselves as victims, and begin taking on the role of absolute authority in their lives.

Little by little you will transform your life by asking "I wonder what this is for?" Gradually, you can begin to see that everything happening *to* you is actually happening *for* you. That's the key question—but you can't get where you want to go if you don't train the mind.

Are you up for this much commitment to your own happiness? I have asked you before: Are you worth the effort? Your response has to be a resounding "YES!"

"An untrained mind can accomplish nothing. It is the purpose of these exercises to train the mind to think along the lines which the course sets forth." ~ A Course in Miracles

Summary
1) Upsets are gold, because they represent opportunities for healing.
2) We are never upset for the reason we think.
3) Resist the temptation to say: I am upset because …
4) There are no small upsets.
5) We are not upset by facts or events. Upsets are the result of our interpretations, and our interpretations are based on the beliefs we hold about ourselves.
6) Want to be 'right' about an upset today? Do not make yourself wrong about that—observe it and smile.

CHAPTER 6

STEP TWO:

Me. It's about Me.

"In the seen, there is only the seen, in the heard, there is
only the heard, in the sensed, there is only the sensed, in the
cognized, there is only the cognized. Thus you should see that
indeed there is no thing here;this, Bahiya, is how you should train
yourself. Since, Bahiya, there is for you in the seen, only the seen,
in the heard, only the heard, in the sensed, only the sensed, in the
cognized, only the cognized, and you see that there is no thing
here,you will therefore see that indeed there is no thing there.
As you see that there is no thing there,you will see that you
are therefore located neither in the world of this,nor in
the world of that, nor in any place betwixt the two.
This alone is the end of suffering."
~ THE BUDDHA

Now we move on to Step Two: "This upset is about me, it's all about me, and it's only about me!" This is perhaps the most crucial step, because without it we're going to do what most people do: blame something or someone else for whatever seems wrong in our lives. We are so used to thinking that we know why we are upset. We believe that certain individuals or circumstances beyond our control are the sources of our being upset:

- We are victims of our parents, families, and/or spouses.
- We are victims of the economy, the government, and the courts.
- We are victims of religious persecution and political corruption.
- We are victims of a polluted environment and/or our own bodies.
- We are the victims of time and history.
- We are the victims of our gender.

The belief that we are the victims of so many influences in our lives, and that our lives happen to us, is a primary belief for nearly everyone on this planet.

But the belief that we are the victims of our own lives is not true — it is a belief. It is a false idea that robs most of us of hope and true happiness. What follows when we see ourselves as victims is an inevitable anger at the circumstances and individuals in our lives who seem to be causing our unhappiness. We need to ask ourselves whether we believe that we are puppets on the strings of our lives—controlled by forces outside ourselves and ultimately by God—or whether we are actually free.

Try to imagine what it would feel like if you believed, at the very core of your being, that every circumstance in your life arose from a creative power residing within you. What if you realized that your experience of life is determined from within, driven by the beliefs you hold about who you are. This collection of beliefs writes the story of your life. The only 'free will' we have is the freedom to change our beliefs and thus our lives. How would it actually feel if you could allow this radical statement to be true for you?

Do you need to tell your story?

Most of the people who come to our center for healing have seen therapists at some time in their lives. The normal commencement of therapy is to tell your story. Then you go back a week later and tell your story again, but very little changes in the process. You tell the story again and again and again, and still nothing changes. The seductive aspect of this method is that you briefly feel better after telling the story: *So glad I got that off my chest, I feel much better now.* Or the other favorite: *I just want to be heard…*

The reason nothing changes is because the real problem is hidden underneath our story. If all we do is repeat our story, then we're actually protecting our core beliefs, making them more real and embedding them ever more deeply in our psyches. To make matters worse, we'll lobby our friends to agree with our story. Often we define a "friend" as someone who echoes our story. When someone commiserates with us, we get to be right about our story. Even if being right is delicious to the ego, it is a huge barrier to a real experience of Love.

We recently had two therapists visiting from another country. We invited them to participate in the circle, after which they commented, "Our work is very similar to what you do. However, we feel it is important that the client is heard and acknowledged. We feel that when a client feels understood, they are ready to move on." In this work, we teach that the suffering we experienced in our formative years is best not explained and understood. That's because the suffering we experience derives from our interpretation of what happened, not what actually happened. Step Two is what sets this work apart from most forms of therapy.

Having spent a little time on Facebook, I'm often struck by the number of "victim postings," as well as the numerous comments from people supporting them. People invariably mention how they too have been victimized in a similar way, so they understand how the victim in the original post must feel. This is a virtual support group. But in my opinion, support groups that don't advocate for constructive change, by way of individual initiative, only serve to support and thereby perpetuate the shared victim mentality.

We may want to ask ourselves, "Is the story of my life worth preserving if it does not bring me peace and happiness?" Another way to ask the same question is this, "Would I rather be right, or happy?" Before I started doing my work, it never occurred to me that these choices were mutually exclusive. I prided myself on being right as often as possible. I could 'win' a debate taking one position in one corner at a party, then go to another corner, take the exact opposite position and 'win' that debate. It did not occur to me that 'winning' was, at a deeper level, losing.

Being right was the juice of life for me. I had the pleasure of being on two juries and in both cases I was the lone voice against eleven others. In both cases I turned the jury around. Sound glorious? It was hell. All that 'being right' made for an incredibly lonely life, and it never dawned on me that underneath that compulsion to be right lay a devastating belief that I was wrong, deeply wrong in the essence of my being. Whenever I treasured being right, the result was isolation and desperation.

When people come for healing work and learn that I'm not so interested in their story, they say, "But if I don't tell you my story, how are you going to know who I am, and what happened to me? How are you going to know what to fix?" The answer is that what always needs to be fixed is their ego's interpretation of their experience. The facts of what happened are always neutral, and can be interpreted in any number of ways. Healing often begins by asking, "Is there another way of seeing this?"

Years ago I was at the house of two dear friends, both therapists, John and Linda. John arrived home for dinner three quarters of an hour late. Before he arrived Linda became very agitated, which she attributed to his not calling to explain. As we waited I asked her, "What is your interpretation of John being so late?" I suggested that her anxiety could be traced to a negative core belief which she wasn't examining.

For instance:

- If Linda had a belief that she could lose love, then perhaps she would worry that John was late because he had had an accident.
- If she believed that she is a victim, then Linda may have thought that John was having an affair.
- If she believed that she is unimportant, Linda may have thought that John didn't call because she wasn't worth the consideration.

Any of these ideas are purely hypothetical interpretations of the neutral fact that John was late for dinner and didn't call. In fact, later processing revealed that Linda's father had been an alcoholic, notoriously unreliable in his coming and going. Consequently, as a little girl Linda had made up the belief that she could lose love at any moment, so when John was late it triggered the same anxiety in her that she had experienced all those years ago. Once such beliefs are cleared, events are experienced as neutral and curiosity will be the predominant feeling.

The story—any event that produces a feeling—seems to explain that feeling, but in fact the feeling is chosen by a prior belief, which is the actual author of the story. Do you begin to see how ridiculously circular the ego's reasoning is? As soon as we feel anything less than love, we can know that we're not in Truth. Truth and feeling are mutually exclusive. In Truth—a state of mind, a state of being, which is not a feeling—we experience only peace. As soon as we feel something else, we know that we've made an interpretation based on our beliefs. It's our beliefs that create the "I" that I made up. The self-made "I" makes up interpretations and having done so experiences them as if they're real and instantaneously forgets it made up the interpretation. It is so important that I recognize that I did the forgetting, that this forgetting has a purpose and that it is this ego–purpose I no longer want or need.

In his book *Man's Search for Meaning*, Viktor Frankl describes his harrowing experiences at Auschwitz, the notorious Nazi death camp. He notes that even in the worst possible scenario—in which absolutely everything has been taken from you—you still retain the freedom to choose how you feel and how you react. As Frankl wrote, "Everything can be taken from a man but one thing: the last of the human freedoms—to choose one's attitude in any given set of circumstances, to choose one's own way." Whether we are in extreme suffering or more ordinary daily struggles, the best attitude to choose is that of the higher Self rather than the self-defeating ego.

Why you must relinquish the story

A woman came to me for therapeutic counseling in Vancouver some years ago. She was thirty-three and had been ritually sexually abused in her early youth. Her story was terrible, about as extreme in its details of abuse and persecution as one could imagine. It took her two and a half hours in our first session just to tell me that story. No doubt she was accustomed to therapists commiserating with her, because when she was finished she remarked, "Over the years I've seen many therapists, and you're the only one to hear the story and not react at all. I can't begin to tell you how freeing that was."

So with that feedback—that she had been liberated on some level by my complete lack of reaction to her story—I received confirmation for one of my therapeutic truisms: *Never believe the story.* If I believe your story, as told, it becomes "real" and we're both stuck with no way out. That's therapeutic collusion, which is not a path to healing. No matter how terrible your story is, what happened to you wasn't terrible per se; it was terrible in your interpretation.

You may notice that I didn't tell her: "Nothing happened" — a typical Buddhist perspective — or "It's just an illusion," or "How did you create that?" I didn't suggest any of these perspectives because to her, the story did happen and was not an illusion. If we want to facilitate healing, we have to work with the experience the client brings to the session.

So after the story has been told, the next step is to say, "Yes, that happened, now what are we going to do with it? Somebody did something to your body; we've established that. Nobody's disputing that. But what are you going to do with it? You've told me your interpretation, which is what actually causes you so much emotional pain. The real questions on the table are: How are you willing to reinterpret what happened, in order to have a normal, happy life? How are we going to help you see that the 'I' in this horrific story is not who you are in Truth?"

What we teach is that there's never any reason to be upset. With Step Two ("It's about me"), blame is relinquished, totally and resolutely, and ownership of any upset reverts to you, where it actually began. Relinquishing of blame and of the story has to happen in order for us to be truly happy.

Here's the challenge: We must trust this step even if we don't believe in it. Without this step, resolution and peace won't happen. "Okay, okay, so it's about me," you have to tell yourself. "I accept that blaming anyone or anything for this upset won't get me what I really want. And what I really want is to be happy, to be at peace." The benefit of taking complete ownership of the upset is to realize that you are always the author of your experience.

I can assure you that when we practice "It's about me," all our relationships are well on their way to being magically transformed. All relationships have the same purpose: healing. Every relationship we have—with food, the air you breathe, your car, or a gnarly customs officer in the airport—is for healing old beliefs. If we are awake, all relationships will offer healing opportunities. If we're not awake, we're likely to have a permanent low-grade irritation, a chronic sense of sadness, or a frequent feeling of anxiety. All day long we're offered gifts, in the form of opportunities to recognize our beliefs through relationship difficulties. We must recognize the cost of 'sleeping' and decide that cost is way too high.

Step Two and romantic relationships

Many couples come to the healing center because they feel that their relationship needs work. While their relationships are ultimately transformed in a very positive way, in the beginning, they are invariably going to be highly uncomfortable. On occasion, couples report that in the beginning of doing this work they feel worse than they ever have.

How could that be? Before doing this work, people can attribute their unhappiness to a wide range of interpersonal issues and never look within. In practicing the Six-Step Process, however, you're addressing the source of all problems—the source is your identity, the "I" you've made up. You are the cause of your relationship not being so wonderful, not your partner. Unless you allow that realization to ring true, you will keep looking for causes and faults outside yourself. Thus, there are two big steps you have to take: The first is to say "it's all about me," and the second is "nothing has gone wrong." Both statements will be a leap of faith, at first.

In fact, there is nothing wrong with your relationship. What's wrong is your interpretation of your relationship, yourself and your partner. When people first undertake this work, they are apt to say, "She should change, and as soon as she does, I'll be happy." And they'll tell her exactly how she should change. But therein lies the error. They are looking at something outside of themselves as being the source of their unhappiness, while the real source lies within; they need to look within themselves and change their minds about who they think they are.

If I insist on being right about my partner needing to change, then I'm stuck with a losing strategy of trying to change her. I'll send her off to enlightenment workshops, I'll send her off to yoga camps, I'll send her off to all kinds of esoteric retreats because, come hell or high water, I'm going to change her somehow. When she comes back all "fixed," then she will finally be the ideal partner for me.

Guess what? That will never happen.

It will never happen for the simple reason that she is already the ideal partner—I just don't see it. What am I seeing instead? I am seeing myself reflected in my partner, and that's what I don't like. When couples come to me for relationship work, the most important and difficult step is for each person to take total ownership of the entire relationship. Many years ago a woman

joined one of our circles in Vancouver and shared a new and exciting idea she had just learned from her therapist that day. She
said: "I learned today that I am 100% responsible for 50% of the
relationship!" That does sound very strong, very powerful. Think
about it for a minute though: 50% of the relationship? How is that
defined and who will do the defining? How long do you think
it would take you to make your partner's 50% larger and larger?

Here's the unpleasant truth: I am not 100% responsible for
50% of the relationship; I am 100% responsible for all of it.

There's no other way to confront how the ego works. The ego
always depends upon the constructs of blame and victimization,
and those are the constructs that typically rise to the surface
in relationship counseling. What couples learn in this Six-Step
Process is to accept that it's all about "me." We have to change
our beliefs about ourselves and if we do, we will have an entirely
new experience—not just in our intimate relationships, but in all
areas of our life.

Our work is not about behavior modification, compromise,
or sacrifice. When I had relationship counseling for my own marriage long ago, it centered on agreements such as: "If I agree to
do the dishes, then you'll take the garbage out." It was all based
on negotiating behavior, and it went absolutely nowhere. If you
find yourself in a counseling arrangement that focuses on
changing specific behaviors—yours or your partner's—then
you'll find that lasting results are hard to come by.

That's because trying to "get your needs met" by another
person will never work. Only you can meet your own needs, and
only by recognizing that a "need" is just the belief that you are
lacking something. That need will never be met because it is not
real! Transform the belief and the need miraculously vanishes
with it. In Truth there is no lack. In Truth we are unchangeably

whole and complete.

That's why our work doesn't focus on behaviors. Obviously, if we are in an abusive relationship or we're self-destructive, those behaviors have to stop in the short term. But everything that's playing out in our relationships is just evidence for who we think we are. To be really happy in life, sooner or later we're going to have to start healing the core beliefs we have carried for so long. There is no escaping it.

The key to Step Two is to be aware that we are constantly looking at our own beliefs when we catalog all the problems of a relationship: "This is me and this is me and even this is me, and I don't like what I'm seeing!" Well, if we don't like what we're seeing, we're going to have to change it—and that means changing our identity. We have to start correcting core beliefs, and if we don't, we're going to be in the same relationship over and over again. Whether we stay with this partner or go on to the next one makes no difference. That's because we're in relationship with the ego-self. But if we're consistently in relationship with our higher Self, extending that higher Self to our relationships, these will be magically transformed.

All relationships are the same

Sometimes people seem to have different qualities of relationship, such as a great business relationship but a troubled relationship at home. This is a situation that can only be sustained for a little while, because the lousy relationship at home is what Papaji Poonja calls the "drop of cyanide in the honey."

If we think we have a wonderful marriage but hate our job, sooner or later that circumstance is going to negatively affect our home life. That's because all relationships are with ourselves. Any relationship we find less than joyful than others represents some troubled aspect of the self. That aspect, or core belief, will keep seeking evidence for its reality, eventually poisoning all our relationships.

A man in his mid-thirties, very successful in business, had absolutely no trouble attracting beautiful women. But after two or three months of dating, those women invariably became increasingly busy and had less and less time for him. They were overscheduled, they had demanding careers, they cancelled dates or couldn't see him for days on end. Sooner or later he always got the message that he just was not all that important. Why did it always happen to him that the women he attracted were sooner or later "very busy"?

As we began our process and he turned his mind to the most recent time when a partner 'was not available' and how that felt, he immediately remembered, "I am three years old, I've stubbed my toe, and it's bleeding a little bit. I run into the kitchen where my mum is making dinner and I say 'Mommy, Mommy,' and my mum turns half turns around and says: 'not now.'"

Right then he made up this belief: Women won't have time for me. And that also meant I am not important or I am not lovable. Thirty years later, he goes to a cocktail party and scans the room; perhaps there are twelve eligible women there, but only one who will eventually not have time for him. Of course, that's the one that he'll be attracted to. If they connect, it's because she has the complementary belief that being "too busy" will protect her from getting really close to someone, thereby defending some wounded story of her ego-self.

We're all beings of energy; beliefs are energy. Our energy field surrounds us and when we connect with other people, it's usually because our energy (beliefs) meets their energy (beliefs). So it is with our fellow at the cocktail party. He will pick, time and again, the woman who eventually will not have time for him. He is looking to live a perpetual replay of that early experience with his mother so it can be healed, but his ego wants to prove that the original story is still true.

It gets more interesting, though. Even if the person to whom I am attracted does not initially reflect my beliefs, over time she will. Let's say I have a belief I will be betrayed, and my new partner is the most faithful person the world has ever known. In that case, I may continually suspect, accuse, nag, and reject her as if she has betrayed me and then, guess what? She will have an affair and my ego will smugly say: "I knew it!"

If we don't like the circumstances that we continue to attract, we can change our beliefs and in so doing, we will attract different realities. There's no doubt that it's challenging to declare: "From here on out I will gladly assume total responsibility for everything that happens to me."

It's a tough decision to make, and to reinforce. Make it anyway!

For if we are willing to make that crucial decision, we've taken the single most important step forward in our own healing. We need to understand that it's impossible to be a victim in the first place, because in truth, nothing that happens can ever really hurt us. It is our thoughts alone that hurt us. It is our interpretation of what seems to happen that causes our suffering. Who we really are, our eternal Self, is unchanged and unchangeable. Because of this, any person whom I'm attempting to blame for hurting me is always innocent. That's a tough concept to accept as well, but it's absolutely essential to our healing that we do so.

Reversing the usual cause and effect

Conventional thinking would have us believe that something happens to us (I am the victim of circumstances) and subsequently there is a reaction, or effect, created as a result of the precipitating cause. My parents not demonstrating love and affection translates to "it's hard for me to show love and affection." Cause and effect, right?

I have learned, however, that how I feel in any given circumstance comes from within, and once I decide that my one purpose, my only purpose, is to be happy, then, guess what? The world becomes a happy place and all the stuff that gets thrown at me is nothing more than neutral events that no longer have the power to provoke or upset me. I have learned how to welcome everything that comes into my life because I understand that nothing can ever really hurt me. I welcome the rain, I welcome the snow (OK, maybe I do not, quite yet). I welcome upsets because I am never a victim. You are not a victim. Not one of us is a victim! There are no victims, only volunteers.

Everything in your life has been chosen by you as an opportunity for your healing. We create our own experience by playing out the expectations that our beliefs have set up. We keep gathering evidence to prove that the beliefs underlying our identity are true. The 'evidence' is the circumstances that we continue to attract, and the underlying beliefs are magnets drawing those experiences to us. For a dramatic illustration of the principle, consider the case of Julie, in her own words:

"I have been raped twice in my life and my interpretation was that I subconsciously drew these experiences to me in order to justify the underlying belief that I deserve to be punished, and bad things should happen because I am unworthy of happiness.

"The second rape was particularly traumatic because the man actually broke into my home in order to rape me. He had my clothes off. I was naked on my bed, and when I realized I was trapped there I pretended I was about to throw up. I jumped up and ran, as if for the bathroom, but instead I ran out the door of my apartment into the hall. From there I ran to the third floor of my apartment building, banging on doors and yelling 'Help! Help!'

"Some girls let me in and they got their boyfriends to go check out my apartment. They came back saying, 'The coast is clear, he's not there, everything's okay and secure, you can go back into your apartment.' And so I went home. At two in the morning I woke up, startled to see the same man in my bedroom again. And this time he was really pissed off, enraged, in fact.

"And he had a big knife this time. So he raped me. I was nineteen, and every night after that I would wake up at the same time—two in the morning—unable to go back to sleep. Clinically speaking, I had post-traumatic stress (PTSD). Thirty years later, I am at Diederik's center in Costa Rica, having just learned the tools necessary to properly process this trauma. So when I woke up at two in the morning at the center, I started processing my traumatic experience of myself alone in my room, using the Six-Step Process.

"I wrote about the trauma, taking the feelings that came up at two in the morning first back to the event, then way back to when I was young. The feelings led me to these beliefs: I am bad. I am not lovable. The world is not safe. I am a victim. Over and over I did my 'forgivenesses' that night and the next day. In the healing circle, I shared what I had done, and that night and every night since then, I've slept like a baby.

"When I first wrote out the story, I could see that I had been losing all this sleep—for what? A story. I hadn't been able to sleep for thirty years because of a story I was carrying around in my head. What happened to me is the story of what happened to a body, and that body is not me. It's not the essence of me. With this realization the trauma stopped tormenting me, and I was finally at peace, and able to sleep."

I don't think it's true that Julie "created" or "attracted" the rapes based on her beliefs. However, the traumatic character of the experiences was chosen by her beliefs. Her ego experienced the rape as punishment, just rewards for the unworthy 'self' she always believed she was. She had made up that self at a very early age, long before the rapes. What made her story so traumatic for decades was her identification with the body. I have worked with countless victims of abuse, physical and sexual, and as soon as the client allows the truth that she is not the body, the trauma subsides. These things were done to the body. We are not our bodies.

I have a body, but I do not identify with that body any more than I identify with my car. I will look after my body, lovingly take care of it by giving it proper nutrients, etc. However, I teach that the body is in the mind—as opposed to the idea that the body is the home of the mind. That is a huge shift in seeing the self, an essentially Eastern way of seeing compared to what most people in the West believe.

Enough of the story
I have said much about 'story' in this chapter and perhaps I need to clarify something: Initially it is important for people to be able to tell their story, simply because they need to know that

they're being heard. There's a trust that develops because of that. But after telling your story once or twice, it no longer serves a purpose. The Blackfoot Indians of Alberta have a wonderful healing circle tradition. Anyone in the circle is allowed to tell their story twice. If they start a third time, everybody turns their chairs around. In other words: "Enough already!" They just don't want to hear it anymore. Why not? Because in the story, there is no way out. Because in the story, I get to be right.

Here is the Choose Again variation on the Serenity Prayer, which may speak to you now after reading the above:

"God grant me the serenity to accept the people I cannot change, the courage to change the one I can, and the wisdom to know that it's ME."

Summary

1) It's about me, not another person. Always.
2) We cannot be victims.
3) There is no one to blame.
4) We are the authors of our own experience.
5) Do not believe your own story.
6) Didn't really feel like allowing Step 2? Don't make yourself wrong. That is the toughest step for all of us.

CHAPTER 7

STEP THREE:
Feel the Feeling

"This being human is a guest house.
Every morning a new arrival. A joy, a depression,
a meanness, some momentary awareness comes
as an unexpected visitor. Welcome and
entertain them all!" ~ RUMI

STEP THREE asks us to note our feelings. Feelings will lead us to our underlying beliefs, which are the barriers to our happiness. We subconsciously choose our feelings based on who we think we are. Our feelings are not the natural outcome of what may be happening at work, at home, in traffic or at the grocery store; we just think they are.

If, for example, you find out that your pre-teen daughter is smoking weed, that is a fact. That you react with anger, worry, horror, sadness, or a host of other feelings is due to your interpretation of that fact. That interpretation is chosen by the beliefs that have been triggered—which may include that you are a bad mother or father, unworthy of parenting, and guilty. We really have no choice, no 'free will': we choose the feelings we experience based on those beliefs. Any feeling we may have, other than perfect peace, indicates that some healing of beliefs is in order. The feelings that lead us to our underlying beliefs are completely insignificant in themselves. The only purpose they serve is to send a wake-up call: "There is work to be done!"

If you were to go sailing in the waters between Vancouver Island and mainland British Columbia, you might see a little red flag in the sea. This little red flag is attached to a spike that someone hammered into a "dead-head." A dead-head is a submerged log. If I'm sailing and I hit a dead-head, there's a good chance that the hull of my boat will end up with a large hole in it, and I will go down with the ship.

The little red flag can be compared to a feeling, the dead-head is the belief underneath. The red flag is not really very interesting, but it is invaluable in avoiding a shipwreck. You have no idea how many times I dead-headed and sank before I started practicing the Choose Again Six-Step Process.

Anxiety (or depression, worry, anger, sadness) is a default setting for many people's feelings, but we don't have to settle for them. If we are willing to continue this process we will discover a way to overcome such debilitating feelings. But the process requires that any upset must be felt deeply.

Many people have no idea what they're really feeling. It's not yet something we're trained (or even allowed) to do in our society. Instead of fully feeling, we are generally taught to suppress what we feel. Even if we are encouraged to feel, then we seldom have the tools to process those feelings. The cause of any feeling we have is habitually seen as outside ourselves, as discussed in the previous chapter. We think we can't help but feel the way we do, because our feelings are caused by outside agents. We cannot change the government, the weather, our partner, or the banking system, so we either commiserate about our feelings, or cover them up. We may do this by eating comfort food, shopping, having a couple of drinks, or taking anti-depressants. When we turn to one of these false solutions, our suppressed feelings and unexamined, underlying beliefs continue to fester like an infection covered by a Band-Aid.

Josie's struggle

Josie, one of our staff members and a former client of Choose Again, came to us as a highly successful athlete with medals, championship titles, and a whole host of emotional issues, including body image. After two years in the medical system, Josie still had a lot of trouble feeling, partly because of a slew of medications, partly because of years of denying her terrifying feelings. As she recalled:

"I had a very easy life compared to other people. I'd always gotten to do what I wanted, and my family supported me so I didn't really have to develop a lot of coping skills. I had always shoved down feelings and never looked at anything. One day I realized that I didn't want to pursue the goal of becoming an Olympic athlete anymore, but I didn't know how to convey that to my family and friends who had great expectations for me. I had been going along with the program, not really looking at anything, until I realized that I wasn't happy with the path I had chosen. When I realized this, I felt as if a carpet had been pulled out from under me. And then I got really scared because I had built my entire identity around being a successful athlete.

"Everybody I saw asked: 'Are you still going to the Olympics?' and I thought I don't want to tell them that I don't want to be an athlete anymore—but I also had too much pride to admit how I was really feeling, so I became anorexic. This was my way out without having to be accountable. Choosing anorexia would enable me to say, 'It wasn't my fault! I'm anorexic, which forced made me to stop being an athlete,' instead of saying 'I'm not really sure I want to be an athlete anymore, and that terrifies me because I've built my entire life around that dream.'

"At that point, I was able to identify my response as part of a recurring pattern in my life. For example, when I was very young I used to figure skate. I remembered thinking, I'm not going to be the best at figure skating; my body is not a figure skater's type. So I quit figure skating without examining any of my real feelings around the issue.

"Because of this pattern, I couldn't just say, 'That's what I'm feeling.' I couldn't just say 'Hey, I need help.' Instead I acted out my fear in passive-aggressive ways, which no one understood, least of all me. I put myself literally at death's door so that family and friends would have to rescue me. All this drama took the focus off my desire to change my professional goals and dreams, which I didn't have the courage to face squarely."

At the age of seventeen, Josie weighed only a hundred and five pounds.

"I went on a crash diet, losing twenty-five pounds in a month. Anything I did eat, about once a week, I threw up. Finally I admitted to my mom, 'I'm miserable and I have to go to the doctor.' The doctor took one look at me and said, 'Oh, you're just depressed. This pill will fix everything.' She didn't ask me how I felt or what was really going on. Her solution was to give me a magic pill that would presumably make me happy and resolve all of my issues.

"About a week later, understanding that pills couldn't address or fix the deeper issues of why I wasn't eating, I realized I needed to see a specialist about my anorexia. A family friend who's the head of an eating disorder clinic at a major hospital in my area agreed to meet with me. But he just gave me a prescription for a new drug, saying 'Okay, now go on this pill, which will work faster than the other anti-depressant you're on.' We didn't even discuss anorexia. Days later I started having suicidal thoughts, which I shared with my mom.

"The doctor had asked me whether or not I was suicidal just a week earlier. At that point, as confused as I was, I couldn't comprehend how anyone could ever kill themselves. Then a week later, I was totally obsessed with swallowing a bottle of pills. I went back to my initial doctor, a woman who had prescribed antidepressants for my friend's brother, who ended up killing himself. So when I told her I was suicidal she sent me to the emergency room at the hospital because she didn't want another suicide on her watch. Psychologically and medically I was very unstable at that point, but I was brought back to some semblance of health and ten days later, released.

"But when I got out I starved myself again and within another ten days I was so dehydrated and so malnourished that I was taken to a pediatric medical ward. They shoved feeding tubes up my nose and again snowed me with drugs. I spent seven weeks on that ward without seeing the light of day. I was having temper tantrums, acting out. Security would come and inject me with a tranquilizer and tie me to the bed. My interactions with the staff became a kind of game. One day I grabbed a bottle of bleach off the cleaning cart and chugged it back.

"So then they put me in the kid's psych adolescent unit, which had a kitchen with some knives. I told the staff, 'There are knives in the kitchen and I'm going to cut myself up with them,' because, again, this was the game I was playing."

Josie's life turned around dramatically when she came to El Cielo and began processing her beliefs. Weaning off the meds allowed her to begin to feel.* Her breakthrough came as a result of remembering early events while completing a Six-Step Process as well as through Holotropic breathing, and also by beginning to recognize her feelings using the Feelings Sheet (Appendix A).

"The early memory that I recognized as having given rise to the beliefs that were running my life was being three years old with a kidney infection. I have a traumatic memory of being on a table with doctors around me putting in a catheter and asking me to pee on the table, which I did. I thought that I'd finished peeing,

---

*NOTE: Choose Again will never tell someone they must come off their meds, and we will never advise anyone how to do so safely. If a client wishes to go off meds, we would first suggest they ask for a safe withdrawal protocol from the doctor who prescribed the medications. If he or she is unwilling to design such a plan then we ask for advice from two psychiatrists who are intimately familiar with our work. They will suggest a safe protocol, and even then the decision is entirely up to the client. Ninety percent of our clients do go off meds, and stay off.

but the doctor told me that I needed to pee some more, which I couldn't do. The procedure was painful and very frightening for me, akin to sexual abuse. I developed the beliefs that there was something wrong with me; that I didn't know my own body; that others had the answers to my problems; and that I must have done something wrong and deserved to be punished. I became convinced that I am a victim and that people are out to get me. The same feelings of people being 'out to get me' may still creep into situations today, such as when I am leading yoga sessions, dating, or leading a circle. I still punish myself with food at times."

Over the years Josie had a pattern of dramatic emergency room visits. When she was seventeen she found herself again tied to a table with tubes being pushed into her after an overdose of Tylenol PM; more recently she had to have intervention for a serious infection. She came to see a repeating pattern due to her belief that there is something wrong with her. That belief is kept in check, and gradually transformed, by being vigilant and processing any feelings that come up. Josie is now a yoga instructor and staff member with a zest for life, and she's an inspiration to our clients.

Josie went through all this just because she couldn't stand to feel her feelings, and doctors cooperated by suppressing them with medications. She didn't examine her feelings in a healthy way as they came up. Here you can see just how important it is that we learn to tune into our most difficult feelings, and even welcome them so that we can follow them to the subconscious beliefs that need to be transformed. There is a school of thought affirming that expressing your feelings is in itself therapeutic.

Expressing your anger or having a really good cry will definitely feel very good—you will likely experience a deep sense of relief —but ultimately it does not correct the beliefs that choose the anger or the deep sadness.

Going straight for the feeling

What everyone learns to do quickly with the Six-Step Process is to ask, "How are you feeling?" rather than "What's your story?" or "What happened?" or, even more deadly: "Why do you feel that way?" So if you're in a relationship and your partner's really upset, rather than letting him or her tell the story associated with the upset ("the doctor kept me waiting for forty-five minutes this morning!") you would ask, "Tell me how it feels; let's get to the feeling." That's because we know that the feeling will take us to the underlying belief, and it's the belief we actually have to work on.

Particularly when you are new to the idea of allowing feelings to surface, it can be helpful to utilize the 'Feeling Sheet' shown in Appendix A, featuring seventy different feelings. Seeing them all written out this way can help you to identify what you are feeling at any given moment or on a regular basis. In Choose Again circles it is usual for participants to select all the feelings that apply to them, and then choose the top three (most intense) feelings to work on. When processing on your own, I would urge you to trace every feeling back to the first time you felt it and what belief has chosen it. Each feeling you have identified on the sheet has been chosen by a belief. They may well all come from the same belief or they may have been generated by a variety of beliefs. It matters not how many beliefs play into any upset. What matters is my commitment and yours to trace them back to the source: a mistaken belief.

If you're on mood-altering medications, chances are you will have a difficult time feeling as the meds are designed to dull the feelings you are running from, a classic vicious circle. The healing work that is undertaken then runs the risk of becoming an intellectual exercise in which real healing is not likely to happen. We must be willing to honestly look at our feelings and we also must be able to access those feelings. We have to be able to feel in order to take the feeling back to the belief, then do the forgiveness that will lead to the necessary transformation of beliefs.

The role of medication

Many of the clients that come to me for healing are on medications, particularly anti-depressants. In all my years of counseling I have only had two clients that I felt really benefitted from being on their meds, as they had severely limiting beliefs which were deeply buried and fiercely protected. What I've found over the years is that typically people aren't on just one medication. There's always a second or third or fourth because the first one didn't work, the second one doesn't really help, and the third one is just adding more difficulties. And so on. One person was on sixteen different medications when she came to our center for healing!

I remember an elderly client I saw many years ago. He was on twelve medications and it quickly became apparent that we were not going to be able to access any true feelings other than the dark blanket of sadness which had become a permanent state for him. After several sessions I contacted his psychiatrist and said: "Mr. Peterson is on many medications and I am not seeing much improvement." The psychiatrist then said a few words I have never forgotten: "Mr. Peterson will never improve!" That statement aroused just a wee bit of passion in me, so I insisted on a meeting with him and our mutual patient. We then heard a by now familiar story: virtually every medication that had been prescribed was designed to ease the negative side effects of the one before. Mr. Peterson is now off all meds and has a vastly improved quality of life.

This is by no means a unique story; it has been played out many times over the last fifteen years. The vast majority of my clients with depression are able to wean themselves off their meds and stay off. Why is that? They learn that depression is a choice, not a disease. They learn that depression is not something that is in their genes. They learn that the real reason for their depression is not that their grandmother was depressed, but they themselves at one point made a wrong choice, a mistaken interpretation, and that choice became the genesis for their underlying negative beliefs. As soon as those beliefs shift, by using the Six-Step Process, the depression lifts.

Anti-depressants are legal drugs prescribed by doctors who firmly believe they will help. And they often do help, initially. It is just a statistical fact that over time, their efficacy lessens to nothing. In fact, over time meds become the problem, and that's because the real issues were never addressed. It's as if I decided to do a line of cocaine whenever I felt tired or sad. I would miraculously feel so much better, almost immediately! That would work for a while, but then I'd need more and more coke to keep going, and the initial 'benefit' would completely vanish. This is an absurd strategy, regardless of the kind of drug.

There is a lot of evidence showing that anti-depressants can lead to suicide, particularly in teens. I have had many clients, including Josie, report that their suicidal ideation began when they started taking their medications. Suicide is even listed as a predictable side effect of some antidepressants. How could a doctor prescribe such dangerous drugs? Not because they are uncaring.

But because they are not informed, grossly overworked, and often have to diagnose patients in seven-minute consultations. Let me be very clear: there is a role for medication. If someone is suicidal or severely depressed or ripped apart by anxiety, medication can bring relief and as such it is invaluable. It should not, however, become life support (or a life sentence) except in very few cases. For pharmaceutical companies the system of drug dependence works brilliantly: shareholders demand profits, and profits are delivered at an obscene level.

Some of the people who come to us for healing have been diagnosed with ADHD, for which they're on medication. Once they are at the center they quickly go off these meds, and find that they really didn't have ADHD. Their symptoms vanish because during their time with us because they're not eating sugar; they're not attached to a computer, smartphone or TV; they're getting fresh air and exercise on a regular basis; they are learning how to meditate—and most importantly, they are healing the beliefs that gave rise to their symptoms in the first place.

In addition to lifestyle changes, the person with ADHD has to find what the purpose of the 'illness' is. Every illness serves a purpose and if you want to heal, really heal, you have to first know what that purpose is—then decide you no longer want it. What purpose might ADHD serve? ADHD conveniently delivers the evidence for numerous core beliefs such as "I am not capable" or "I don't deserve to be happy."

"The pain is there; when you close one door on it, it knocks to come in somewhere else..." ~ YALOM

Many years ago I had the great privilege of facilitating a circle of teenagers at an inner city school. At one point I asked the kids in the circle what the worst thing that had ever happened in their lives. These kids came from unimaginable difficult 'home' circumstances: Mother prostitute, father dead; mother dead, father in jail; mother in jail, father abusive. You get the idea. So when I asked that question I expected to hear a variety of issues tied to life circumstances. One young woman, fifteen years old, immediately raised her hand and said: "The worst thing that ever happened to me was the day I was diagnosed with a learning disability."

Not quite what I had anticipated!

"Would you say a little more about that?" I asked.

"The day I received that diagnosis I was given permission, or actually encouraged in a weird way, to never try again."

One client we have is a woman in her early forties who suffers from debilitating pain. There is no medical explanation for that pain, tests have not showed a physical cause, and she is desperate. When we started helping her look at the 'payoff' from that pain, she quickly realized that when she was little, the only way she ever got attention from her busy professional parents was to have an illness. That belief masked an underlying belief of simply not being lovable at all. She experienced great discomfort, and had sought medical relief for her symptoms over and over again.

As a culture, we abhor discomfort and will inevitably seek outside ourselves to alleviate it. Our intolerance for pain and dis-comfort feeds addictions of all kinds. But in order to do truly deep healing work, we have to feel, and that can be uncomfortable. If we mask our feelings (physical or emotional) with meds, drugs, online obsessions, or shopping, we will not allow ourselves to receive the gift inherent in discomfort. We must be resolutely vigilant and become aware of our feelings at all times, even the tiniest ripples of irritation. Seven hundred years ago the great

Sufi sage and poet Rumi said: "If you are irritated by every rub, how will your mirror be polished?"

Feelings and parenting

How important is it for parents to be aware of their feelings and own them? Children typically feel responsible for their parents' moods and feelings, so it is vitally important to let children know, at all times, that whatever we are feeling has nothing to do with them. Our children do not make us happy or sad; no one does. We choose the feelings we experience! So if we get in the habit of sharing our feelings with our children, and teach them how we process these feelings, then we are demonstrating that we take 100% responsibility for what we're feeling, and we are teaching them to do the same. They'll soon see that they are not the cause of anyone else's feelings, freeing them to do the only job they have at that time: to be a child.

I would also want to teach my child that his or her worth is intrinsic and cannot be changed. His or her worth doesn't increase by getting great grades, nor does it decrease by smoking pot or making dumb mistakes. Because their worth is intrinsic, they have absolutely nothing to prove either way. It isn't their job to make me happy; it isn't their job to keep their mommy and daddy together; it isn't their job to make peace in the family. Their job is to be kids. And their destiny is to fall in love with the Self. The way to teach that, of course, is by demonstrating it yourself.

It is important to be at peace whenever we address children. A productive, meaningful conversation won't happen without that peace—in fact, the opposite might happen instead. If the parent is not at peace, the child will automatically take on the dis-ease of the parent. She'll make it her fault, and then shut out that parent. You may have noticed that whenever you blame anyone, be it a child or your partner, they tune out. They just do not want to hear it. They just do not want to feel, once again, that they are the cause of your upset, because they already feel just that at a deep level.

How do you feel when someone lays a guilt trip on you? You don't enjoy it, you may tend to recoil, withdraw or defend. Our children don't enjoy it either. Kids and partners do not like to hear the accusatory "you." They will listen, however, to "This is what's going on for me." Then they can see that they're not implicated in whatever it is you're bringing up.

A conversation about feelings is very useful for everyone to practice around the dinner table, or in the car on the way to soccer practice. Parents can talk about what happened to them that day and how it made them feel: "My secretary made a sloppy mistake and it cost me an account; boy, was I pissed off! I really wanted to blame her, I even thought of firing her, but then I took a deep breath and I realized that my anger had nothing to do with her mistake, or what that mistake cost me. My anger is always about something I've made up about myself!"

Imagine showing up with your feelings to a seven-year-old. Once you remove the word 'you' from your vocabulary, kids listen. They'll be riveted because of your honesty about what came up for you. You'll have demonstrated that you own your feelings, regardless of the story you're telling. Of course, you would have to continue the process and show that you were able to regain your sense of peace after that upset. That is what it means to be a parent.

True parenting means teaching our children to take full responsibility for all their feelings and actions, by leading the way as a role model. By the way, it's also important to convey to our children that everything that arises is an opportunity for healing, and in this sense, nothing ever "goes wrong." Everything is an opportunity for healing and learning. That's a very exciting idea!

About ten years ago I was working with a couple who were in turmoil. They believed they hated each other and wanted a divorce. In one or two sessions we were able to clear some limiting beliefs (or at least become aware of the devastation they caused in the marriage), and things began to turn around for them. The husband had begun meditating; using meditation as a tool to help him still his mind and find inner peace.

One day they brought their two boys—four and five years old—to a session. These kids acted like little beasts. They ran around the room, making noises and distracting everyone. That night, the father was meditating at home, when the four-year-old, who had a slightly warped sense of humor, blew up a paper bag and popped it by his father's head. To say that dad was a little triggered is a clear understatement. The dad lost it and sent the kid from the room.

The next morning the child came down to breakfast and said to his father: "Daddy when you were upset last night, that wasn't really about me, was it?" He had learned in the counseling session (in which he had seemingly not paid any attention!): that he was not responsible for his father's anger. The release one feels when no longer taking on someone else's upset is huge.

That is successful childrearing. That is successfully raising children to know that they are not responsible for how somebody else feels. Now, of course, the next step is also for the child to look at why he needed to pop that paper bag in his father's face. What was he looking for? Probably punishment; that is, he was looking for a reaction from his father consistent with the belief he already had about himself (that he was a problem child). Whatever the exact belief, that has to be examined and processed also: What were you thinking when you blew up that paper bag? Was there something about your dad meditating that annoyed or upset you in any sense? How do you feel when you see dad meditating?

A little word of advice for those with teenage children: Don't enter a fight with a teenager—it's a losing proposition. The teenaged brain can't follow a logical argument. Instead, talk about feelings. Thus, if I'm in a conflict with my teenager, I'm going to say, "Here's what I'm feeling, and here's what's coming up for me… I'm interpreting your skipping school (or drinking, or whatever else is going on) as my fault! I look at your behavior in a way that says something about me: I must have been a bad father. I must be a bad person. But I know none of that is true. Your behavior is not a reflection of me."

The Truth of me cannot be that I'm a failure as a parent, or a failure in any sense. I need to be in touch with the higher Self in order to maintain my peace, and I should not enter into a discussion with my teenager if I am not at peace. Only when I am calm and have done my own work, only then can I expect good results from asking my teenager how she has been feeling lately. "How does it feel to skip classes and be sent to the principal's office?" How she feels will lead to a belief and the next step is to help her heal that belief.

In any difficulty with a child, my first job is to ask myself, "What am I feeling? What is coming up for me? What do I believe about me right now in this situation? " If I do that honestly, my child will respond because he'll know I'm not accusing him, or holding him responsible for what I'm feeling.

Above all, be honest about your feelings. Don't hide them and do not make them important. They have no meaning other than "little red flags." And second, never indulge your feelings, do not sit in them like a dirty bath, do not wallow. Do not be 'patient' with your feelings. Why would I be 'patient' with feeling like shit? Don't be patient, be intolerant of feeling less than gloriously happy. Don't be patient and do not judge! Use the feelings for the only purpose they have: healing and joining.

"A human being is a part of the whole called by us universe, a part limited in time and space. He experiences himself, his thoughts and feeling as something separated from the rest, a kind of optical delusion of his consciousness. This delusion is a kind of prison for us, restricting us to our personal desires and to affection for a few persons nearest to us. Our task must be to free ourselves from this prison by widening our circle of compassion to embrace all living creatures and the whole of nature in its beauty." ~ EINSTEIN

SUMMARY

1) You must feel the feelings in your upset. You have to "feel it to heal it."
2) Own the feelings at all times.
3) We choose our feelings based on who we think we are.
4) If you are on medication, you may not have easy access to your feelings.
5) Allowing feelings and processing them with children is great parenting.
6) Do not be tolerant or indulgent with your feelings. Use them!

CHAPTER 8

STEP FOUR:

Remember My Ancient Feelings

*"Discomfort is aroused only to bring the need for correction
into awareness." ~* A COURSE IN MIRACLES

FOLLOWING from Step Three, now that you're "in the feeling," you commit to recall the first time you felt this particular feeling—the earliest memory of that feeling. Use the present feeling in order to remember the first time you felt that same way. We're talking about the feeling triggered by a current event, not the event itself. Close your eyes and allow the feeling of the moment to guide you back to an early childhood memory of a formational incident. Give yourself the space to explore it: How old were you when you first felt this feeling? What was happening then? Who said or did what? It doesn't have to be a hugely traumatic event; whatever memory comes up is the right memory to process now.

Remember: You are never upset for the reason you think. The feeling of aggravation that comes up for me when I'm in the express line of the supermarket—where one is supposed to have only ten items, and the person in front of me has twelve—is the same feeling that might arise within me when someone doesn't return my phone calls. "How does that work?" you may ask.

Well, because the feeling is chosen by the same belief that was triggered by each event. That belief (in this case perhaps: "I'm not important" or "I don't matter") was formed in an incident that happened long ago, and it is the memory of that incident that we're after.

When I ask a client "Is this a familiar feeling?" the honest answer is always "yes." It might be a "No" only if you are absolutely convinced that "it's about someone else." It has to be an old feeling, even if not familiar, simply because we do not 'make' new feelings after age eight or so. If it seems to be an unfamiliar feeling, it could mean that the belief that spawned this 'new' feeling has been deeply buried for a long, long time. Remember my own experience of coming face to face with the belief that 'I should not have been born'? To recognize that "yes, it's a familiar feeling" allows you to recognize again that the current circumstance is not the cause of the feeling. By acknowledging that, you are ready to let go of pursuing resolution in the story and to go much deeper, to the root cause of the upset. We have learned that the story doesn't matter. Whatever is happening now (not in form but in content) only seems to be happening now, it is actually just a replay of an ancient event.

The story simply allows you to keep feeling what you're used to—or rather, addicted to. In a very real sense, the dealer for my addiction hides in my story!

Let's look at sadness. Like all feelings, sadness is caused by a complex mixture of biochemicals. Every time you experience this sadness, a specific combination of biochemicals is released in your body, thereby reinforcing the feeling. When this happens regularly, you become addicted to those biochemicals, and thus to the feeling that sends them into your system. This biochemical reaction was established the first time you ever felt that feeling, and thus literally became a part of you.

The feeling of sadness is a red flag indicating that a mistaken belief about your self is at play. After noting it, immediately get to work. After becoming familiar with the Six-Step Process, you'll be able to link feelings to beliefs via memories quickly, in a matter of seconds. In so doing, you'll nip that particular biochemical pattern in the bud, very much like putting a glass of wine down after one sip or walking away from an enticing waft of cigarette smoke.

"The initial corrective procedure is to recognize temporarily that there is a problem, but only as an indication that immediate correction is needed." ~ A COURSE IN MIRACLES

If you choose not to do an immediate correction, however, you are choosing to 'use.' You are allowing certain feelings to take over simply because your body misses the biochemicals and is actually experiencing a craving for them. Anyone who has ever given up an addiction knows what this craving feels like. Because you won't feel quite right without that particular biochemical rush, you'll soon be back to choosing sadness. You're an addict, plain and simple.

On the other hand, if you don't continue to see yourself as a victim (or whichever belief is at play, choosing your sadness), you can resist the craving, find the belief, do your forgiveness (Step Six), and your sadness miraculously vanishes. In order to heal your addiction, you must find the belief that has been triggered. The belief is the real 'dealer' as it chooses our feelings. After you've identified the main feeling ask, "Where does that feeling come from? How old was I when I first felt this very same feeling?" And in doing this, realize again that what you're currently feeling has nothing to do with what just happened.

In the example above, my angry reaction has nothing to do with the fact that my phone calls were not returned, nor with that person in line at the grocery store— even though my ego is screaming that I know exactly why I am upset! The first time I felt that feeling was when a sudden breeze caught my mother by surprise, she accidentally slammed the door, and I awoke with a shock. I am simply replaying my upset three-year-old 'self' every time I am presented with such seeming 'evidence' of not being important.

Never feeling safe

Julie came to the center for healing as a last resort—she had been considering suicide. She found enough hope with us to keep on going, and to keep coming back for more healing.

"One of my predominant feelings was the feeling that I was never safe. One day, as a young woman in my late twenties, I had an appointment with my gyne-cologist. When she was examining me she told me she saw something unusual—a polyp or something—and she wanted the doctor to have a look at it, which of course I agreed to. However, the next thing I knew the doctor was cutting inside me and all of a sudden I had an image of myself at the age of two, in the bathtub, in a great deal of pain. In a two-year-old's voice I said to the doctor, 'Stop, stop, you're hurting me!'

"In my mind's eye I then went back to an early, deeply buried memory of my mother abusing me in the bathtub. I was shocked as the pieces fell into place. The abuse from her was a violation, one in a long line of them that I was to experience growing up."

Julie experienced two traumatic rapes later in her life, but this memory of abuse by her mother was the key to her healing. Sometimes those memories are deeply buried, like Julie's, and at other times you might be surprised at how quickly you will access the memory associated with a particular feeling.

"I am invisible"

A few years ago I had the pleasure of dining with an old friend with whom I used to drink and play sports. On this occasion we were at a wonderful Japanese restaurant, enjoying a lovely meal and some sake.

He turned from his drink and said to me, "This work you do is really just BS isn't it?"

I smiled and replied, "Maybe."

"What's it really all about?" he pressed on, vaguely interested.

"Well, it's about finding a path to real peace, real happiness."

"Oh, I don't need that," he quickly told me.

"I'm so glad to hear that," I answered back. (Yes, I have been accused of using feather-light sarcasm at times). "So you are always at peace?" Now, I knew full well that he was not. He worked twelve hours a day making more money than he could ever spend, and was riddled with anxiety.

In any event, he assured me he was always at peace. Just at that moment, in the Tatami room next to us, a cell phone rang, shattering the quiet, relaxed mood of the restaurant. Upon hearing it my friend said, "That really pisses me off."

I took this as an opportunity to get to work. "This feeling of being pissed off," I wondered aloud. "When and where did you first feel that?"

Without missing a beat he replied: "I am four years old, in Ireland, and my little sister has just peed in the corner of our living room."

I continued: "What was the message you may have given yourself about you at that point?"

His reply was classic: "I am invisible and I do not matter."

This belief of unworthiness was why he felt compelled to be in professional overdrive, earning increasing amounts of money to prove that he was not, in fact, invisible, but rather a real force to be reckoned with.

Does this ring any bells?

The roles of parents

One of our counselors, Ted, suffered feelings of utter devastation when his female friend of many years did not want to enter into a romantic relationship with him, but rather chose to date another man. By following these feelings back, Ted retrieved a memory of being five or six years old: "My parents had decided to go out to a formal ball instead of spending their Saturday evening with me. Up till that time, my parents were always at home and available to take care of me. I couldn't understand why they would want to go out. I felt completely abandoned and devastated by their choice to go dancing, leaving me at home with a baby-sitter. I couldn't understand it at all!"

There are times when it may be very difficult to access the memory that triggered a belief and subsequent feelings, and sometimes a parent can supply the missing information. A man came to see me about ten or twelve years ago. His life was going well in most areas but he had one problem: he couldn't eat in public. He couldn't eat in front of anybody. As soon as he was in a relationship, the idea of having dinner with his partner was unbearable. As you can imagine, that put a little crimp in his style. So we spent some time looking at where this may have come from. However, we couldn't find the genesis of his problem, which we can usually uncover in a session or two. This was not an affliction you will find in the DSM5, yet.

So I asked, "Is your mother still alive?" He told me she was. I said, "Do you think she might be willing to come to a session?" He said he would ask her. She showed up at our next session and I asked her, "Would you tell me about your son's first few days and what was happening for you at that time?" She proceeded to explain that she had become pregnant by a man who had left her. She subsequently met another man whom she ended up marrying. However, there was a problem with her new husband: he was pathologically jealous of the natural physical closeness between her and her newborn, and he forbade her to breastfeed the baby.

How did she deal with that? Because she couldn't breastfeed in public, she breastfed her baby in secrecy, in private—in a closet. No doubt she experienced a high level of anxiety, hiding to sneak the feeding of her newborn son. As a result, in the first days of this baby boy's life, he picked up the message: "Eating in public is dangerous."

It's important to see what belief this boy/man had made up around this issue. He picked up on his mother's fear, and her fear became his fear. He developed an instinctual belief that if he ate in public his life would be in danger. Thus, eating in public literally became a life-and-death issue for him. Neither the mother nor her son had made that link before. But in our work together, the minute the link was established, the forgiveness was completed and the problem resolved. The man could eat in public, because the danger was gone.

When life gets too serious

About ten years ago a man in his early forties was referred to me by a colleague. She had worked with him for a few months but then referred him to me because they had reached an impasse. He was deeply depressed and there appeared to be no way to budge his depression. He was a financial analyst based in New York who worked hard at his job and made a lot of money. But there was clearly no joy in his life.

He sat in front of me, in a cloud of grey: his face was grey, his clothes were grey, and his energy level was a deep grey. He said: "I am clinically depressed. What are you going to do about that?"

My reply to him was: "Depression is an interesting choice. Why do you think you are choosing it?"

At this he became agitated. "I am clinically depressed! My father was clinically depressed, and my grandfather was clinically depressed! I guess you didn't hear me the first time?" It took the rest of our first session together to have him even consider the possibility, however remote that might seem to him, that depression just might be a choice he was making.

In the second session we started to explore feelings. Because of his depression, he was unaware of his feelings other than an all-pervasive dullness. We then did our first Six-Step Process and here is what it revealed: When he was a little boy, about three years old, he was playing in his parents' garden and found a beautiful beetle. Eager to share his find with his father, he ran into his dad's study. His father was a prominent brain surgeon, a very serious man, whose study was a very serious place. It contained lots of important looking-books, black leather furniture, and not a lot of color.

This happy little boy ran into his father's study shouting

"Daddy, Daddy, look at what I found!" His important father, who was sitting at his important desk, turned around and raised one eyebrow. That was it. The child's elation was deflated and all of the joy he was feeling in that moment drained out of him. And this is all that it took for this little boy, now a middle-aged man, to be absolutely clear that joy was not to be a part of his life. He got the message loud and clear. Or, rather, he made up that message loud and clear—because his father hadn't said a word.

He and I proceeded to do a few more Six-Step Processes around this issue. I saw him one more time after that, and three years later I received a beautiful card from him telling me he had gone back to university, became an elementary school teacher, and was working harder than ever for a fraction of what he'd earned before—while feeling happier than he ever thought possible.

His clinical depression, once diagnosed as "treatment resistant," had lifted entirely. His joy in life had been restored to pre-beetle levels.

Getting past denial

Sometimes people are afraid to look at their feelings, and develop a habit of denying them. They may say, "My life is great! I was upset, but it's okay now," and they want to leave it at that. I suggested to one woman that she notice her feelings by writing them down on a daily basis, because she was tending to gloss them over in the group. This practice eventually revealed memories of her mother comparing her to her sister. Throughout her life, she needed to prove to her mum that she was good enough. This woman realized that she was still trying to prove to her mom that she was good enough—hence her very successful business. She'd spent her life compensating for feeling not good enough by being better than anyone else.

Before we move to Step Five, don't forget to check in with the level of emotion you are feeling in the memory you have retrieved in this step. Go into the memory and make a note of how big that feeling is, on a scale of one to ten, as described in Chapter Four. You'll need to review this number when you have completed Step Six.

By now you may feel a little overwhelmed by all this information (I just cannot resist: "Is being overwhelmed a familiar feeling?"). I appreciate that this is a lot of radical information to take in. Hang in there, for this is your ticket to freedom. This work will take you to a very powerful place.

Summary
1) The powerful feeling of the moment can always be traced back to an early, formational incident.
2) You are never upset for the reason you think.
3) We become biochemically addicted to repeating powerful feelings.
4) The more serious our feelings, the more likely they are to be denied or "diagnosed," instead of us taking responsibility for them.

CHAPTER 9

STEP FIVE:

Establish My Judgment of Myself

"Beliefs are the unquestioned acceptance of an idea in the absence of verification and reason." ~ WU HSIN

W E'VE SEEN that by tracing our feelings back, we can retrieve memories of a precipitating incident or series of incidents in which those feelings first arose. In this chapter we will look at how these memories hold the key to understanding how we constructed a particular erroneous belief that is running our life today.

Here is the process so far:

- We've acknowledged that we're upset;
- we know it's about us;
- we're focused on the feeling;
- we've remembered the first time we felt this way.

Now what? As we remember who said or did what, we ask ourselves: "What did that say about me? What was my interpretation of myself at that moment?"

Whatever that interpretation was, it was wrong.

This is the time when every ego quickly wants to forget about Step Two ("it's about me") and shift back into blame or rationalization of the feelings. At this point I often hear: "I felt that way because what my Mum said really hurt." In other words, the ego has commandeered the process and moved back into the familiar territory of explaining, blaming, and defending. Whenever you hear yourself say: "I felt that way because…" you know you have run away from owning your upset. That means you will not experience the transformation of core beliefs that we are after.

Go into the memory and assess what judgments you had about yourself at that time. Here are some of my own judgments:

- I am not important.
- I am not lovable.
- I am not supported.
- I don't matter.
- There is something wrong with me.
- I don't belong.
- People can't be trusted.
- I should not have been born.

And the ubiquitous one:

- I am unworthy.

Because these beliefs were created in my formative years, they stuck. They formed the lens through which I viewed my entire world, and they could still run my life to this day if I let them. For example, I may notice that:

- I get nervous when someone is angry (and yet, I surround myself with angry people).
- I hate conflict (and yet, there is conflict all around me).
- I have trouble trusting people (and yet, I attract people who cannot be trusted).
- I get anxious when things are not going according to schedule (and yet, I will sabotage any schedule).

- I am hurt when someone is late for an appointment with me (and, yet, I am rarely on time).
- I am afraid of walking into a room full of people (and yet, I am petrified of people's opinion of me).
- I need to know the schedule (and, yet, I almost compulsively ignore schedules).

All such tendencies are triggered by ancient memories kept in place by my beliefs. It is as if what happened seventy years ago, in my case, is happening right now. There are so many little or seemingly insignificant incidents that can provide the genesis of a limiting, erroneous belief. As we've discussed, these beliefs then run the rest of your life like a default program.

"Each day, and every minute in each day, and every instant that each minute holds, you but relive the single instant when the time of terror took the place of love." ~ A Course in Miracles

It's very important to remember that the "traumatic" events that create beliefs are not necessarily traumatic at all. They are made traumatic by the ego's interpretation! And these events don't have to be anything seemingly dramatic (like incest, concentration-camp imprisonment, or murder). Any event that causes our child-self to create a debilitating belief, or set of beliefs, is a force to be reckoned with. We have found over the years that the number one most common cause for negative or limiting core beliefs is a seemingly innocuous event: "My father was five minutes late picking me up from kindergarten." It is shocking, perhaps, to suddenly come face to face with the awareness that the cause for my crippling, life-long beliefs was something as meaningless as this.

Processing upsets

Recently at El Cielo, there were two seemingly very different people in the healing circle. One was Carol, a 19-year-old from a middle-class family, with legal and illegal substance abuse issues. The other, David, was a highly successful accountant in his late 40s who had risen to a global leadership position in a multinational firm of accountants. Both came to the circle visibly upset, and they each engaged in the Six-Step Process to uncover their hidden beliefs.

Carol's feeling of being victimized, triggered by a trivial comment that someone made at breakfast, led her back to the memory of her brother's friend exploring her body when she was five years old. Later, he sexually abused her for years. From that memory she made up the belief that she was weak and powerless, and frequently found herself seeking evidence for that belief by choosing relationships in which she would be victimized. Her belief also led to her being powerless over substances.

David, triggered by being let go from the job that he loved, due to circumstances beyond his control, followed his feelings to a memory of his days at a boarding school in England. He had absolutely no control over his fate there, and felt completely powerless and fearful of punishment. The only way to stay safe in that situation, he felt, was to excel academically and to take as much control as possible so that others could not get him into trouble, the consequences of which were invariably extremely painful. Corporal punishment in the form of caning was still used liberally at that school.

His belief that he was weak and powerless led to a life constantly driven by a need to be in control, propelling him up the corporate ladder. While David's expression of his belief "weak and powerless" may look more sensible than Carol's, neither one of them was happy. Both would be intensely triggered or upset by any event that reproduced feelings of weakness in them.

Watching them process their beliefs together, which at times may be done in pairs, was a sweet and poignant moment. David's upset around his job loss dissolved, and he was able to see it as a neutral fact that said absolutely nothing about him. Carol returned home and put an end to a relationship that had not served her well—her boyfriend had also been her dealer.

One of my clients, Pamela, came to see me one day, upset that she had been yelling at her kids. She wanted to stop but felt so frustrated whenever they ignored her or refused to pay attention to her, so she always ended up raising her voice. I asked if there had been someone who did not listen to her when she was young. It turned out that her mother, who was deaf, could not hear her when she was just beginning to talk, as an infant. This led to immense frustration for her as a toddler, so she made up the belief that she was not important, or else her mother would have understood. That belief triggered an angry response from Pamela whenever she perceived that someone was not paying attention. So she behaved in a way that vindicated her belief: constantly putting herself down, or putting others ahead of her.

After processing that belief and recognizing that she'd always had an intrinsic worth, she reported back months later that she had not yelled at her kids in quite some time. She was not even tempted to yell any more. That's how it works. When the belief is corrected, it no longer induces the behavior that will validate it.

One of the Choose Again counselors shares the following story of how she developed beliefs that subsequently ran her life:

"Once when I was about three or four, I was dressed in a frilly little summer dress and put on top of the woodpile at our cottage at the lake. My father wanted to take a picture of me with his new movie camera. For some reason I decided that I didn't want my picture taken and I said so. He ignored my request and took the picture. I started to cry and the other people watching started to laugh.

"In this critical moment, probably meaningless to my parents and siblings, I decided that I was weak and powerless and that people laugh at you if you are weak and powerless. I made up those beliefs and have been gathering evidence to prove that they were true most of my life. I built an entire personality around these beliefs and never once stopped to question their validity. So many times my friends and family were actually laughing with me, but I couldn't see beyond my built-in perception that I was weak and powerless and therefore a laughing stock to be ridiculed.

"Many years later I was invited to question these two beliefs. When I did a 'reenactment' of the story the adult me saw clearly that I was neither weak nor powerless, but simply a little girl making an interpretation based on very little knowledge of herself or her situation."

From events to beliefs to behaviors

One client at El Cielo, Judy, a young woman of eighteen, not only ate a vegan diet but could hardly stand to have her food cooked in the same kitchen or eat with non-vegans. The subject of her dietary extremism came up in circle one morning, and through the Six-Step Process she revealed a memory from when she was very young, around two years old. She and her sister were playing with a delicate bird's egg. Her sister had found the egg in a nest and it was very special to her; Judy was allowed to hold the egg and accidentally broke it. At that moment she felt as if she had not only broken her sister's heart, but also murdered the bird that would have hatched. Her response was to make everything better by taking care never to harm another living thing, and so she became a vegan.

The incident had given rise to beliefs that Judy had destroyed love, could never be punished enough, and that she was monstrous. These beliefs had played out in a variety of ways, one of which was substance abuse; that is how she punished herself. This example shows a very clear link between the precipitating event, the beliefs that formed, and a person's subsequent behavior. Other examples may be less obvious.

Beatrice came to me admitting that she often felt acute embarrassment in social settings. By focusing on that dreadful feeling for a few seconds, she retrieved a memory from a family holiday when she was about four: "We had taken a trip on the Hispaniola to a Treasure Island, and my brother and I were digging in the sand looking for coins we'd been told were buried there. Suddenly out of the bushes came a gang of three pirates, pointing their guns at us and demanding that we put our hands up. I was terrified! I put my hands up as quickly as I could and everyone started laughing. I was so embarrassed that I hid my face in my mother's skirt when I realized that the pirates were not real, and that everyone was laughing at me!"

Beatrice felt stupid and very embarrassed, feelings that solidified into beliefs that were still playing out in her life some forty years later. The belief that she was stupid drove her to prove herself by jumping through higher and higher hoops, getting one professional qualification after another, but never feeling any satisfaction from having done so. Nothing she did to prove herself was ever good enough.

The benefit of looking back at childhood memories as an adult is that it is so much easier to see how ridiculous the resultant beliefs are. Beatrice was able to laugh at the memory, realizing that the other people on that beach were laughing because of how cute she looked with her hands up and a shocked, frightened expression on her face. She could easily see that she had not been stupid, just delightfully, childishly innocent. There was no cause for embarrassment—she was only four! Still, our ego minds make up ideas that drive our behaviors and feelings until we recognize the patterns and set about undoing them. This example also shows that our beliefs arise from all kinds of situations—they can be funny and seemingly trivial as this one, or as traumatic as physical, emotional or sexual abuse. The results can be devastating regardless of the perceived magnitude of the actual precipitant events.

The memory that Peter accessed by following his feelings of anger seems quite insignificant. Yet it led to a belief that got stronger and stronger, as it gathered more and more evidence, until Peter believed himself to be the epitome of evil.

"When I was about four years old, my family went to Hawaii on holiday, leaving me behind with my grandparents. Later I saw the photos and they obviously had such a great time without me. Why didn't they include me? Surely they would have, if they loved me, and if I wasn't 'trouble'. So I made up that I was trouble, that I was unlovable, that I was bad. Throughout my life, even when faced with evidence to the contrary, such as doing well in school, I would sabotage the positive and turn it around. So at school I wouldn't do my homework;

then I would fail and be in trouble with my teachers. I spent a lot of time in the principal's office, and with each occasion I was cementing my belief about how bad I was, how deserving of punishment. Eventually I got to a point in my life where no amount of punishment and suffering was enough to assuage my guilt. The evil that I thought I was demanded more and more evidence, until I lost any idea of ever having a happy life completely.

"My suffering got deeper and deeper until one day I discovered my girlfriend had hung herself in our apartment. I believed I was responsible and that I had actively killed someone, my self-hatred was so intense. That was the point at which I found Choose Again.

"When I came to Costa Rica it took me about two weeks to even begin to 'settle' in and then one day I felt an unfamiliar feeling—that of looking forward to something: the weekly soccer game! From that point on, with the help of Holotropic breathing and processing, I began to feel happiness that I had not experienced before. Because this initial, tentative level of happiness was so much better than the place I used to be in, I accepted it as good enough and didn't allow myself to go any deeper into my healing. I returned to my home town and soon discovered that I had only scraped the surface. There was much, much more work to be done. So I applied to return to the center in Costa Rica as a volunteer. I was accepted and after a long, profoundly impactful training I was invited to become a full time staff member.

"Now that I am back as a counselor I recognize the importance of vigilance in catching any thought that is not a loving one, in order to maintain my commitment to absolute peace. Now I find the most important idea is to recognize that there is never a reason to be upset. Recently, I was doing the accounting and had just finished balancing the books when someone came in with $2000 worth of receipts. This person knew that I had been working on the accounts, so I felt justifiably pissed off. Because of my vigilance, I was able to take just a few minutes to remind myself that no one can take away my peace; that is a choice that only I can make. It didn't take long for my peace to be restored."

As Peter's story reveals, our core beliefs are extremely powerful regardless of how they began. So, what's the way out? Well, we must retrain our mind, and retrain it rigorously. An untrained mind can accomplish nothing. You made up your beliefs and you are the only one who can undo them. It's that simple. We have to become extraordinarily disciplined with our thoughts. We have to learn to meditate and to watch our thoughts at all times.

"The well-disciplined mind should only speak when requested to perform a task. Untrained, the mind becomes an unruly "onstage" performer and a nuisance. The self needs to learn respect for the Self and the silence of the Presence. By observing the mind, it becomes apparent that the self represents the disruptive, unruly child who constantly seeks attention." ~ DAVID R. HAWKINS

Mind training helps us to recognize and intercept thoughts that would lead to unhappy results. If we don't do that, the ego —a false idea of ourselves—will continue to run the show in our mind the way it has for years. It won't change because it is doing exactly what it wants to do. We have to intercept ego and say, "Ha! There's a thought of scarcity. There's a thought of not enough love. There's a thought that I'm not supported, or there's a thought that I don't belong." If we're vigilant about watching our thoughts, we can catch the erroneous ones before they can do any more damage. And then we must correct them, using the technique discussed in the following chapter.

SUMMARY

1) Any upset at an early age can become the seed for a core belief.
2) The judgments we have about ourselves at a young age become our controlling beliefs.
3) Our beliefs can be discovered in early memories.
4) Discipline is essential. Be vigilant with your thoughts.

Chapter 10

Step Six:
Embrace the Absolute Truth about Me

"I am larger and better than I thought.
I did not think I held so much goodness."
~ Walt Whitman

So here we are at the last step of the process. We have noted our feelings and how strong they are on a scale of one to ten. We've remembered a formative incident, and have identified one or more erroneous beliefs, which have been driving our patterns of behavior, and which have been triggered by this latest upset. Now it's time to correct those beliefs so that we can reclaim the happiness that is our birthright. How do we do that? We utilize the two-part forgiveness process described in chapter four and explored further here.

We need to correct our beliefs one at a time, so choose the first belief that arises. Let's say you're feeling angry, and one of the underlying beliefs that you have identified is that "I am not important." When you are in the memory of that emotion (let's say that your mom or dad wouldn't let you have the toy you wanted), submerged in the angry feeling triggered by that belief, take a deep breath and say out loud, "Forgive me for believing that I am not important." Respond with, "Thank God that is not true! I made that up long ago. It is just a belief that does not serve me.

I can now let go of it." Pause. Take another deep breath.

In Choose Again circles these "forgivenesses" are said while looking into someone else's eyes, and that person then responds. This has been shown to be effective because we are using the eyes of the other as safe witness to the truth. When we look into someone else's eyes, we see our Self reflected. When that person then repeats the forgiveness back, the person who is doing the process has no trouble recognizing the innocence of the other person and thereby learns to recognize the innocence in themselves. It is, of course, possible to do these "forgivenesses" alone—out loud or in your head. It can also help to use a mirror. This process was intentionally designed to be done on your own. To become free of outside help is the goal.

The second part of Step Six is to confirm the Truth of you, which is done through another round of forgivenesses. This time seek to forgive yourself for forgetting the truth about who you are by saying, for example: "Forgive me for forgetting that my worth is intrinsic." This time your response would be, "Thank God that is the truth" simply because, yes, you had temporarily forgotten. Who you are in Truth has never changed and is patiently waiting for you to remember. The real essence of you is simply waiting for you to say it's time to pull back from the story and reconnect with the Truth—to recognize who you have always been. That's embracing the Truth of who you really are.

It is immensely inspiring to observe people who have a very powerful, convincing belief that their worth is zero begin to accept that their worth is intrinsic. They think they have no worth, or that nobody loves them and that they'll never be loved, they'll never be seen, they'll never be recognized. When they get their mind around the fact that their worth is intrinsic and unchangeable —and they really take it in and accept it—it's truly amazing to watch their faces. At first their immediate response is: "That's not true." To which we respond, "I recognize that it does not feel true right now, but how would it feel if it were true? What would that feel like? What would the experience feel like if that was actually true?"

Then they say "Well, that would be incredible." So then we reply, "Well, then live accordingly. Live from that premise: My worth is established by God — it's intrinsic — it's unchangeable."

I had one client who was so convinced that the audacious statement "I am innocent" didn't apply to him, that whenever I would say in a circle "You are unchangeably innocent in Truth," he would ask "Do you think that applies to me too?" He had been put into foster care as a child; his dad was an alcoholic. Throughout his life he had collected vices which he attempted to solve, unsuccessfully, with various Twelve Step programs. He reports feeling much lighter now, as he allows himself to connect to the Truth of himself. He used to cry a lot at circles, an indication of the connection to his True Self.

When the first round of forgiveness is complete, check in again: Go back to that moment when you first felt the anger and see what your level of anger is now. Has your anger gone down? How do you experience that moment now? How do you feel when you go back to being four years old and your mum or dad wouldn't get you that toy? If the upset initially did not go down, it could well be that we are dealing with another, different belief, which you must also then trace back to its source and process as well.

You must commit to continuing this process until the original upsets rates at zero. When you have done this you should be able to look back at the events that were occurring in the memory retrieved in Step Four, watching the replay in your mind calmly, without any emotion. If you can, then this round of processing has worked. If there is still some emotion left in the scenario go on to ask yourself for forgiveness for every belief you made up at that time.

Here is a chart of typical beliefs and the forgiveness formulas that can correct them:

BELIEF   **FORGIVENESS**

Victim I am part of Oneness — it is impossible for me to be a victim. I am the author of every aspect of my experience. I have chosen absolutely everything that seems to happen to me. This idea is a huge stretch for all of us in the beginning and only becomes acceptable when I really accept that nothing ever goes wrong — that everything has always been for me.

Guilty, I am 'bad' I am unchangeably innocent. My worth is intrinsic. I cannot change it no matter how much evidence to the contrary the ego drags in. Imagine a trial with the ego as a corrupt prosecutor dragging in inadmissible evidence — but the court has long since declared my absolute innocence.

Unloved I am love. There is only Love. There is no alternative except in the ego's deluded mind.

Worthless My worth is established by God, not by what I do or don't do — not by what I say or don't say, not by getting more degrees or dropping out of school. Let go of trying to prove how worthy you are because it will never work. Only intrinsic worth lasts and provides the security we always seek so feverishly.

Separate, alone   I am whole and complete, part of Oneness. There is only the Self. There is nothing outside this Self. I am never alone.

I deserve punishment   I am innocent. I was taught that if I was punished enough, eventually I would be admitted to "heaven." Not so. I am already in heaven; punishment is sought only by the ego to prove its faulty beliefs.

Stupid   I am part of Oneness — it is impossible to be stupid. The only 'intelligence' is divine intelligence, and that we share with all the universe. My IQ has nothing to do with living my birthright: to be happy!

Powerless   The power of love is infinite and has no opposite.
Monstrous   I am love and that is all I am.

The result, when I have completed these "forgivenesses," as long as I have correctly identified the offending belief, is a sense of peace, calm, and happiness. Many clients report a feeling of lightness associated with undoing the burdens from the past. Here are a few examples from my practice and those of other Choose Again counselors:

A 70-year-old woman who had grown up in an orphanage found that she had a strong belief in scarcity. She felt that she never had enough money. When she processed her upset around money she recalled a terrifying memory of how, as a young girl, she had polio and was in an iron lung fighting for air to breathe. Her "aha!" moment came as she realized that all her life she felt she was fighting to get enough money, but really she was still fighting to get enough air. She had developed a belief that "there is not enough for me." The lightness resulting from healing that belief was noticed and commented on by her family and friends.

An elderly gentleman who had also been a foster child had a sarcastic wit that hurt people deeply—they'd keep their distance so as not to get hurt by his sharp tongue. It took several workshops and private sessions before he plucked up courage to tell me that at age fourteen, he had persuaded two boys living at the same reformatory into some sexual experimentation. Since that day he had been drowning in self-hatred. He believed that he was unlovable and unworthy of being around other people, so he needed to be kept separate. He had effectively imprisoned himself by using hurtful speech to keep others away. After he processed his self-loathing and became aware of this pattern, people really noticed the difference in him. He no longer needed to be so nasty to everyone, and started feeling close to people for the first time in fifty three years.

Jennifer had a particular problem saying goodbye to people. She would cry all the way through funerals or goodbye dinners for employees. It got so bad that she would avoid all such situations, but didn't want to miss important events. Through Six-Step processing she discovered memories of her baby sister, born with some of her internal organs on the outside of her body, for which she was in and out of hospitals for surgeries. The client made up the belief that it was her fault that her sister had to be in hospital, i.e., if she had been a better big sister this wouldn't have happened. She also felt abandoned because of all the attention her sister received. In her three-year-old mind, she'd abandoned her sister as well. By forgiving herself for believing that she could be guilty and abandoned, Jennifer's experience at funerals changed. She was able to attend without crying at all and, at the same time, feel a deep love for the deceased and their family and friends. Her life changed and there was a noticeable new lightness about her.

The initial sense of peace and even euphoria that accompanies successful processing is often not permanent, so we have to be vigilant with our thoughts. That's because the ego sets out to reinforce old beliefs as soon as we finish processing. This happens because the ego is that set of beliefs. It will defend the beliefs that comprise it, protecting and reinforcing them at every turn to ensure its very survival. If my ego has been telling me several hundred times a day that I am bad, guilty, stupid, alone, and a victim, it is unlikely that I will make a permanent change in those beliefs with just one round of processing. However, each time I catch an upset and process the beliefs that are triggered, those beliefs become weaker and the attacks less destructive.

Forgiveness

The best definition of true forgiveness, I think, is that of Brent Haskell who states in his powerfully clear book, *Journey Beyond Words*: "Forgiveness is just the awareness, beyond your thoughts, of the meaninglessness of all that seems to cause you pain."

The thoughts that cause us pain are the thoughts that arise from the beliefs we hold about ourselves. None of these are true. Being told that the pain you have lived with for so long is caused by a meaningless event may initially be experienced as offensive, and does require a bit of a leap at first.

Forgiveness is a process that leads us to recognize that our worth is intrinsic. Forgiveness in this process is never about what we did or what somebody else did. In the Choose Again Six-Step Process, forgiveness means remembering that we are unchangeably innocent. We forgive ourselves for believing that the identity we made up is actually who we are. Forgiveness in this process is to recognize who is the 'I' that chose to be hurt, or chose to feel rejected, or chose to feel abandoned? That 'I' is not who you are. Forgive yourself for forgetting who you are.

Forgiveness in this context, then, is not about forgiving the actions of someone else. I'm not forgiving my father for beating me, but I'm forgiving myself for believing that the message of the beating was that I'm bad. The fact that my father had a highly unpredictable temper was not my fault, even if every single member of my family told me that it was. I am not responsible for the feelings others choose, any more than others are responsible for the feelings I choose. The belief I formed about myself was mistaken and does not serve me. In recognizing that I made a mistake in developing a belief that I am guilty, I also recognize that my father is innocent too—he was simply acting out his own beliefs. Seeing him as innocent will actually help my own healing as we have shown in Chapter 3.

This same example illustrates a fundamental teaching of the Course, that everything we witness in others is either an extension of love or a cry for love. My father hit me three or four times a week for years. Now what was this really about? I can either frame it this way—"He was a son of a bitch, I hate him"— or this way: "I must have been a really terrible kid, otherwise he wouldn't have done that. I hate me!" That makes me feel guilty, so then I will act on those guilty feelings by acting out to create additional evidence for my guilt.

Or, I can see his behavior as a cry for love, which then opens the door to an entirely new interpretation. Then, being beaten didn't say anything about me. It tells me that he was in a lot of pain. But I can only see this when I am at peace. If I'm not, then I'll have to deal with my own cry for love first.

Every word out of my mouth, and every action taken, can be judged in only one of two ways: as a "cry for love" or an "extension of love." Can we make it any simpler?

> *"Teach him that whatever he may try to do to you, your perfect*
> *freedom from the belief that you can be harmed shows him*
> *that he is guiltless." ~ A Course in Miracles*

I am not forgiving the harm done to me, I am forgiving the belief that I could be harmed.

Please realize this form of forgiveness does not condone bad behavior. If my teenage son smashes his bedroom door in a fit of rage, then his anger must first be processed along with any reaction to the incident. Processing will neutralize the emotion so the broken door can be dealt with as just something to be fixed. I would present it as an opportunity to find healing that has been clearly called for. After that healing, the neutral facts will be looked at dispassionately: "How are we going to fix the door?" My son may have to pay for the damage, but this is not punishment for his behavior—it is a consequence of his actions and the loving thing to do.

Forgiveness versus Punishment

Our culture functions on a punishment or reward system in which we're constantly judged. If we're good we get a reward, if we're bad we get punished. As a result, we're always in search of punishment for our guilt. This is the exact opposite of the idea of forgiveness expressed in Step Six, which shows that we are unchangeably innocent. We're unchangeably whole, and unchangeably loved, and there is nothing that we can do to alter that. We're neither good nor bad—we just are. Our behavior is a result of our beliefs, and in order to change that behavior we have to change our beliefs about ourselves.

We're addicted to the feelings associated with punishment and so we punish ourselves mercilessly with our thoughts. Someone who has just done something that is absolutely terrible wants to hear that they're guilty. That's why they did it. They want to have that experience; they want the guilt and they don't want to hear about forgiveness, they only want to hear about punishment. "How long am I going to be punished for?"

One client from Holland was really upset about the fact that he wasn't going to be punished indefinitely for some of his previous behavior. In fact, what he told us in the healing circle was, "I can't get out of this without getting punished." The irony is that he *is* being punished relentlessly by his ego thoughts, which have produced a "life sentence" of unhappiness. That will continue until he can accept the concepts of forgiveness and innocence.

Another client was a recovering addict and a murderer who had spent many years in jail. He came to one of my workshops with his girlfriend, who was also in recovery. Before he came, he said, "I don't want anybody to work with her except you, will you guarantee me that?"

And I said, "I think I can guarantee that." When he went for lunch, his girlfriend started into a process with one of the other staff members. Upon his return, not seeing his girlfriend with me, he asked, "Where is she?" and I said, "Well, she's doing a process with Carolyne." And he went ballistic. He said, "I could kill you, I could rub you out like a dog, and it wouldn't mean a thing."

And he was convincing. He had spent most of his adult life in jail and did not see going back as a deterrent to an angry impulse.

I turned to him, made eye contact and said: "You cannot hurt me. I love you, you cannot hurt me." I said it three times, and he collapsed and started to cry. For the first time in his life he had a visceral experience of what it means to be truly innocent.

> "The word 'innocence' means a mind that is
> incapable of being hurt." ~ Krishnamurti

Had I been afraid, if I had actually believed that he could hurt me, we would have had a potentially serious problem. But I was not afraid. At that moment I knew who I was, and fear had no place in my eternal identity. Of course he could have killed my body, but at that moment, I was very clear about my identity as Spirit.

Innocence is who you Truly are. Innocence is a quality of being which is intrinsic and unchangeable. If you present me with a Charles Manson I will sit in front of him and say, "You're absolutely innocent." He won't like that. Why not? Because his whole identity is "I'm a monster. Don't tell me I'm innocent." Every one of us has done things we are not proud of, some relatively bad, others not so bad, and some just plain silly. When 'guilty people' hear that what they've done has no impact on who they are, they become quite disturbed initially, but ultimately experience tremendous relief.

The Choose Again Six-Step Process provides the tools necessary to recognize and deconstruct our erroneous beliefs, in order to once again live in the true innocence of your Self. When you practice these precepts regularly, all your relationships are radically changed. That's because all your relationships are with your 'self', and you are now transforming that little "s" self to the big "S": the eternal, universal Self. In so doing, you fulfill your inherent potential by living a life of purpose—the one that is your birthright, the one you were truly meant to lead.

That's why this work is so effective for many "problem" areas, including depression. Depression is a growing epidemic, but it simply means depriving oneself of love. It is not a disease, it can not be 'cured' with a pill. Somewhere along the way, either consciously or subconsciously, the depressed person has decided not to let love in. If you don't let love in, you will not know who you are. On the other hand, when you let love in, you know who you are. You are love. In Truth, you can only give love and receive love. How many of us are aware of the fact that we 'block love' in our intimate relationships? How many of us are aware of the impact that choice has on the quality of intimacy we experience?

One client had been seriously depressed for a very long time. She had tried everything and was willing to try anything to be rid of this condition, which was preventing her from furthering her academic work, and was stressing all her family relationships. It only took two sessions to completely turn her life around. She used the Six-Step Process to discover that, as a little girl, she had made up a belief that there was something wrong with her. Her willingness to look at that belief, realize that it was not true and let it go, led to immediate and dramatic change. Months later she is still enjoying her new-found happiness, telling everyone she meets about her miraculous cure! Her readiness for a change, and willingness to use a new way of thinking, allowed her rapid healing.

By the time we have finished Step Six, we have acknowledged the Truth about our Self. In this acknowledgment—and the perceptual shift that comes with it—lies the power that Truth can actualize in our life in positive and meaningful ways. This is the path to lasting happiness.

"You are the Essence of the Essence,
The intoxication of Love.
I long to sing Your Praises
But stand mute
With the agony
Of wishing in my heart!"
~ RUMI

SUMMARY

1) Forgiveness is the process by which the beliefs that make up the small 's' ego self are diminished, so that our awareness of our big 'S' Self can grow.

2) We need to forgive ourselves for our mistaken beliefs (who we think we are) and for forgetting who we are in Truth, in order to reclaim the happiness that is our birthright.

3) Keep processing and transforming negative beliefs until your emotional reaction is down to zero.

4) This forgiveness process does not condone bad behavior — we are not forgiving the behavior of others or of ourselves.

5) The ego will start to reinforce old beliefs again unless we remain vigilant with our thoughts.

6) Above all, do not make yourself wrong. No one I know has been perfect in applying these steps, so please resist the temptation to judge yourself.

CHAPTER 11:

Family Dynamics and the Six-Step Process

*"Nurturing our own minds will also affect those around us;
we will benefit family, friends, colleagues, and society in general."*
~ GESHE TASHI TSERING

"Do not try to change the world, but change your mind about the world." This universal teaching suggests that you are in charge of your experience in the world. Understanding this, you are removed from the 'victim' role, establishing you as 'author' of your dream, rather than just the one experiencing your dreams. "Does changing my mind actually change the world?" you may ask. Well, for most of us that may seem like a tall order. But the idea allows you a different interpretation, a new way of seeing what you believe to be happening. It is in that shift in perception that your entire world will change.

I have also found that when I do my work—when I process my mistaken beliefs—many others in my life seem to be doing the same. We often hear from clients that after they've been to the center, "I went back to work, and people have changed so much while I was away."

That is what we refer to as the ripple effect of our work. When one person heals, many around her may seem to be healing at the same time. That is pretty wild but we have seen it happen over and over. Some of the effects of this are seen and visible, and some are not.

An analogy to this universal, societal healing is the healing that takes place within the family unit because one family member has begun healing work. The healing of one person's dysfunction can very often become the catalyst to bring dramatic healing to the family dysfunction of the whole. It tends to brings increasing self-awareness and heightened consciousness to other members of the family who then, in turn, begin to see the role they have played in forging a family dynamic which, in the past, led to strife, conflict, depression and a host of other symptoms. One member of the family comes to us, says "ouch," and that "ouch" is a cry for help on behalf of the entire family.

When I began my practice I worked primarily with youth suffering addictions and other negative behaviors. Invariably, parents would arrive at my office and proceed to tell me that their children were in some sort of trouble and needed "fixing." Parents generally want their kids to behave in a certain way, get good grades, go to university, or find employment. These certainly seem to be reasonable desires. Very often, however, that desire is fed by feelings of guilt or unworthiness. Parents want their child to be evidence for their worth. If, however, the child has other ideas and it looks as if the parents' pre-ordained path might not be followed, then parents sometimes reach out for help to get their progeny back on the "right" track. It is a fearful thing for most parents to have a child that does not conform to societal norms.

Whenever a parent comes to see me about difficulties they are having with a son or a daughter, I will invariably suggest we start doing some healing work with the parents before we even think of talking to the child—even if the child is clearly making choices reflecting self-hatred. What needs to change first is the parents' perception of the problem. If the parents are willing to process their own fears, beliefs, and lack of self-love, very often their child's behavior will also change as a natural outcome. There are a number of reasons for that.

First, all parties in this story are part of a family system. The child's core beliefs—that he or she is not good enough, for example —demand evidence to be reinforced. The parents' core beliefs —perhaps also about not being good enough—need evidence as well, which the child's behavior amply provides. The child's cry for love is being met by the parents' own cry for love, so conflict ensues. If the parents succeed in addressing their own issues, then they will no longer need to cry for love, but can extend love instead. As the relationship of each parent to himself or herself is transformed, the relationship between parent and child changes naturally, often at surprising speed.

Second, if the parents do their work and gain an understanding of who they are in Truth, that everything is for their healing, and that nothing ever goes wrong, then they can be much calmer when faced with another night of drinking or drugging or binging and purging, whatever the problem of the child might be. Then a child's inappropriate behaviour is no longer seen as 'wrong,' but as a cry for love. When a parent does not react negatively to their child's behaviour, he or she will no longer reflect the guilt the child is looking for as evidence of their own unworthiness. In other words: the parents have stepped out of the action-evidence-reaction cycle. This prevents the child from feeding her guilt addiction, so the evidence of his or her badness no longer mounts. The underlying beliefs are then not being fed.

Third, the child will see the change in his or her parents and will be curious about what has caused that change to happen. They may be curious enough to want to try it too. This happened on many occasions. I'll tell you about one of them.

One woman, Karen, brought her daughter Joanne to see me and explained that Joanne was a total mess—she had been anorexic, was now bulimic, was drinking, smoking, and taking drugs. She was leaving the house at all hours of the night to go to raves in distant towns. She had virtually dropped out of school in grade nine. I managed to convince Karen, the mother, to come and see me to work on her own issues, which she did weekly for a couple of months. By using the Six-Step Process regularly, she was able to get off the anti-depressant medications she had taken for over twenty years. She started exercising and looking after her health in ways that she would not allow herself time to do before. Her strained relationship with her husband was transformed and Joanne reported that she felt better, knowing that she was no longer able to drag her mother down with her when she was out of control.

It took a few years, but Joanne eventually agreed to come to the center in Costa Rica and stayed for a few months. While she was with us she learned how to experience joy without needing substances. By healing her core beliefs, she was able to turn her life around completely.

It is interesting to note that Karen was so happy to shed her depression that she brought her husband Jack to see me. We worked on his stress levels; he was a top executive in a multi-national firm. Shortly after he learned the Six-Step Process he took on a global position which he would not have been able to manage previously, because of the enormous stress load and the problems at home.

I even met with Joanne's grandmother, who had been quite traumatized by her granddaughter's behavior. She needed to do a lot of work around her own sense of worth, and reported that our sessions helped her in all sorts of unexpected ways—even just dealing with previously awkward social situations.

Joanne's brother John, who had left for university and stayed away afterward to escape his dysfunctional family, returned after nine years, seeing how much everyone had changed. He had been having a battle with depression, so he and his wife came to see me. Both report vast improvements in their relationship and in their own happiness.

I feel so privileged to work with families because it is usually family dynamics that generate core beliefs in the first place, and it is remarkable to see the results when whole families work on their healing together.

Many years ago a young woman named June came to our healing center in Costa Rica. The month before arriving she had undergone ten electroshock treatments. She had been prescribed twelve different mood-altering medications and, as you can imagine, she was a mess. Her psychiatrist had basically thrown up his hands in despair—there was nothing left in his toolbox he could suggest with any reasonable hope of success. In addition to a huge smorgasbord of meds she had indulged in street drugs, mostly cocaine. She was not present, her eyes were dull, her spirit virtually broken and her will to survive was flickering at a very low pitch.

But there was something to work with: anger. She was angry at herself, at the world, at her parents, and at her partner. While it is clear that in our work anger for its own sake is not a very useful emotion, in this case it showed me that there still was a fighting spirit, even if the fight was directed at herself and mostly self-destructive. Her stay at the center was memorable. Rarely had I seen an ego so committed to self-destructing without actually taking the last, irrevocable step. She demonstrated every day how the ego will resist healing—how the fear of Love is really the only fear there is, and how she was absolutely determined to preserve her self-made identity at all costs. It was an epic struggle between her loving Self and the self she had made up. In the end the Self won. Her parents both came down and spent time with us learning our process, and learning the new language their daughter had begun to master. After June went home to be with her family in an entirely new way we learned of the remarkable 'ripple effect' story, which came out of this healing.

Her mother had not talked to her brother (June's uncle), in twenty-five years. However, once June's mother was exposed to the healing work that we do and began to understand the power of forgiveness, she too started reaching out. She decided to call her brother to extend love. They had a wonderful, loving conversation and during their talk she happened to recall that their father had died of colon cancer. So she asked this long-estranged brother, "Have you had a colonoscopy lately or at all?" And he said, "No I haven't." And she urged him to do so.

Shortly thereafter he had the colonoscopy and its results revealed that he had colon cancer. The disease was at a very early stage and because it was caught so early, her brother recovered fully and has been clear of any signs of cancer ever since.

That is one of the enormously gratifying aspects of this work: we have no idea how far the healing ripples can go. But we trust fully that they will go far, and keep having an ever wider effect on more people and families. To me, this story epitomizes what can happen. Strange as it may seem, families of the people who come to the center often resist healing and transformation, because they feel a powerful pull to maintain the status quo. To change family dynamics requires commitment on the part of more than one member, if it is to be successful. The family often reverts to dysfunction because it is what all parties are used to; they know how to handle that, however miserable it may make them. I want to be absolutely clear that this is not out of malicious intent, but simply because the ego/family system naturally resettles in a familiar pattern. This is paradoxically called the 'comfort zone' of the family, although very little true comfort is found in that state.

Allow me to shed some light on this puzzling phenomenon. The person who has been 'selected' by the family to be the black sheep has become the symbol of their guilt. He or she is the walking mirror reflecting the deeply held belief in guilt shared by the entire family. Now, if this person were to heal and no longer be evidence for the mistaken belief in guilt that the other family members sustain, they will have to find a new mirror to remind them of their painful beliefs.

Once we are aware of this 'status quo' tendency and have made a genuine commitment to continue our healing no matter what, miracles happen. Families are transformed and generational hurts are healed. Ancient hatreds and feuds are re-interpreted and forgiven—and that is why everyone who works with me is so passionately dedicated to this work. We have seen so many seemingly hopeless situations turned around, so many broken relationships returned to Love, so many lives get back on track and that is our greatest joy.

The first step begins with you. You are so worth it! Commit to a year of really committed awareness and processing. One year, that's it. You probably cannot imagine the enormous, healing shifts that will inevitably happen in all aspects of your life. All for the better!

CHAPTER 12

Six-Step Mis-steps

"Wisdom begins when a man finds out that
he does not know what he thinks he knows." ~ PLATO

THE SIX-STEP PROCESS is an extraordinarily effective way to remove barriers to love, thereby increasing happiness in those who choose to use it. There are, however, a few pitfalls to be aware of. The ego's very survival is threatened by this process. It is sly and even vicious in its endeavor to reassert itself. Here are the most common challenges:

1) Justifying feelings

Do not stray from Step 2: *Me. It's about me.* I cannot emphasize this enough. Do not fall for the temptation to "justify" your feelings. It is so easy and tempting to admit that you are upset (Step one) only to immediately tell yourself or others why you are upset. The justification "I am upset because...." is not easy to shake off, and yet that is what you have to do. Without mind training, you have no idea why you are upset; you just think you know so you can immediately move into the territory of "I am right." The trained mind remembers: "I am not upset for the reason I think," and then begins the necessary inquiry into which belief chose the upset.

Once you have undertaken the process and accepted Step Two as essential to your release from a mistaken belief, do not allow yourself to slip back into the story. The story has only one purpose: to hide the truth and allow you to continue to protect a core belief. You are not your story, you just think you are. You made up the story, then forgot you made it up. Remember that the self who made up the story is not who you really are!

2) **Beware the spiritualized ego!**

The spiritualized ego knows the right language, can quote spiritual platitudes with the best of them and can smile under any circumstance —even while seething. The spiritualized ego is not interested in doing the work. Why would it? That would bring about its demise. It is hellbent on protecting its image. There are many examples of this little creature at work; here are a few:

- "I felt ignored by her, but I know that was just a cry for love on her part."
- "Ah, your mother died? Oh well, just remember you are not a body and she wasn't either!"
- "I hear you are getting a divorce, I wonder how you created that?"
- "He yelled at me, attacked me verbally in the most horrific fashion, I was terrified, but I know he is innocent."
- "When you did that, you made me feel absolutely worthless, but I know I am innocent."

Please note the seductive quality of the spiritualized ego: it is always justified in its pain and suffering, always right that it was someone else's doing, and always ready to state the spiritual cliche: "It's all just an illusion." That last line is really important to intercept. If you are upset in any way at all, it is not an illusion to you at that time. It is real to you and unless you do your work to own the upset and process it, you have merely joined the multitude of spiritualized egos that march in lockstep to the tune of "it is not real, it doesn't matter" etc.—not a good crowd to hang out with.

3) **Using the work as a weapon**

Couples who are familiar with this work can sometimes use it as ammunition against each other. It is not uncommon for a couple who have temporarily forgotten who they are, to angrily challenge one another: "What are you believing? You know this is about you!" This is like a red flag to a bull.

You can only help another to process what is going on with them if you are at peace yourself. Only when you are truly at peace can you ask that important, loving, question: "Tell me how you are feeling? You are believing something that could not be true. What do you think it might be?" Never enter into a discussion or process with someone who is upset unless you yourself are at peace.

Another way to use this as a weapon is illustrated by this story. Many years ago we had a young man in our Youth program who seemed to take to the work, said all the right things and made seemingly genuine progress in many areas. One day I got a call from his dad, furious at me. "What is this garbage you are teaching my son?" I asked him what happened and he told me the following: "I work hard, I am a welder, I do not make tons of money. I had saved up for a brand new pick-up truck which I need for work and paid for it with cash. My son took a spike and ran it the length of the truck and when I exploded the little bastard had the nerve to say: "You seem very upset, that is your process..."

You get the picture? That is both a spiritualized ego in full flight and someone using the material as a weapon.

4) Using "I am innocent" as an excuse for bad behavior

This is a tricky one. We've had more than one person at the center with a substance abuse issue who would say, "I can now go back home and do a line of coke without feeling guilty." No! This is a dramatic misunderstanding and abuse of the work. If you know that you are innocent, if you know who you are in Truth, it would not even occur to you to engage in an activity or habit which could only spring from self-hatred. I used to drink myself into a stupor most nights for thirty-plus years; that is self-hatred in action. Now I do not have to fight against drinking; I do not have to resist the temptation. Drinking to excess is anathema to me now. The "I" whom I now know myself to be does not even consider that level of abuse as an option to fight against.

5) Settling for merely "better than before"

This is what I call accepting the proverbial "7" of happiness on a scale of 1 to 10.

This is a common pitfall. When I owned a restaurant many lifetimes ago, I learned that "good enough" was never good enough, and it is the same with this work. If you were a -236 on a 1-10 scale of happiness when you started, and now you are a 2, the ego may tell you "well done, that is good enough." Do not fall for it. You deserve to be fully happy; that is your birthright, claim it! Settling for 7 is not safe; the measure of unhappiness you are allowing yourself will start growing again, and before long you may find yourself thinking of ways of ending it all. Vigilance and discipline—two dirty words to the ego—deserve your full commitment. You are so worth it!

6) **Processing while not 'in the feeling'**

If you do not connect to your feeling to trace it back to a belief, and instead rely on your thinking to seek out a situation from the past, then you are undertaking an intellectual exercise that will not work. Intellectually it makes absolutely no sense that I would feel responsible for the WWII camps I grew up in—but feeling revealed that insane belief (see Appendix B: Holotropic breath work).

7) **Using the ego mind to repeat forgiveness formulas**

If you are simply speaking from ego when you say, "Forgive me for believing I am unlovable" while still inwardly telling yourself, "You're full of shit. It's not true. You're a fraud!" then you'll notice that the feeling does not shift. The process depends not on the words that are said but the intention behind them—which must be to hand over your beliefs to your higher Self.

8) **Frustration that processed beliefs return**

Do not underestimate the addictive quality of guilt. Like all other feelings, it can generate a biochemical addiction. I know a lot of people, including myself, who can go for a long time being really nice and loving, then do something not so nice. Why? We need a fix. We want to get a little shot of my bio-chemical cocktail called "guilt" in order to reinforce old beliefs.

The ego will inevitably seek ways to sabotage your healing unless you remain vigilant with your thoughts at all times. This is the ongoing challenge of the work. The important thing is not to let lapses become another reason to beat yourself up and provide evidence for your lack of worth, stupidity, or any other negative belief of your choosing. I use the phrase "Awww Honey" whenever my ego acts up and starts telling me what a hopeless case I am. It is an effective way of taking away its power over me. Beliefs can be tenacious little beasties. My belief that I am not supported still kicks in from time to time… or so I have been told by those who love me ("… or pretend to love me," my ego quickly chimes in).

Be patient. This work is not an instant fix, a pill, nor a magic elixir concocted by an angel just for you. This is a method for changing your mind. There are no pills that "cure" depression any more than there is a drug which will make you permanently happy. If there were, we would be idiots not to rush out and buy it, all of us. Be patient, and be gentle with yourself when you fall backward, as you almost certainly will. Do not make yourself wrong. Be prepared to go through the Six Steps over and over, and then again. So often I have heard people say: "I did that process yesterday." Yes… and? A belief that is only weakened is still there. Get back to your process immediately.

Be impatient, too. If you're feeling lousy, why would you be patient? Do not pass "GO" till you feel great. Do not wallow in feeling sorry for yourself and have your ego tell you: "I am working on it." Be aware of when you are feeding an old belief, a nasty old wolf, an addiction. So be kind, but impatient. Don't beat yourself up that once again you got triggered—it happens to all of us. Just get back to Step Two.

Implications and Applications
of the Six-Step Process

YOU HAVE taken the time to read this little book and you may even have started applying some of the teachings. If so, you've probably begun to glimpse the immense potential benefits of using this process. In closing, I would like to suggest some areas where the Six-Step Process is likely to have an impact.

Children and the Education System

This is a a realm of prime importance. If we can start kids off knowing that their worth is not determined by outside opinions, by grades, or by the clothes they wear, we will have laid the foundation for a truly peaceful planet.

I look back at my own school experience as one of horrendous and virtually continuous conflict, starting in the second grade when I returned to Holland from Indonesia. While I had to fight a gang of kids every day in Jakarta because I was white, when I came to Holland I continued to fight—often the entire school in a wide circle surrounding me at every recess—simply because I was 'black'. After having lived in Indonesia for eight years I was considerably darker than my Dutch schoolmates. My self-hatred was fully developed, founded on profound guilt over the years in camps, and I was an extraordinarily disruptive element.

In Holland I was immediately at the bottom of the class in all subjects, the teachers hated me, and the students felt no different, with one or two exceptions. One day some people came to the school and gave us a series of questions to answer. Shortly thereafter teachers treated me dramatically differently. I was invited home to some of the more popular kids in my class and my grades soared; I rose to the top of the class in a very short time. Later I learned that I had scored very high on an IQ test, and people were impressed. As they were impressed, which I experienced as approval and love, I did very well in school.

It did not take long, however, for my core beliefs of guilt, shame and self-hatred to come back in full force, and once again I began to self-sabotage on a grand scale. My core beliefs demanded evidence, and doing well in school, as well as being liked, was not congruent with my self-made identity. If the teachers and I had been able to use the Six-Step Process the teachers could have processed their intense dislike of the disruptive influence I was in the school, and I would have been able to process my self-hatred.

Bullying

There is no doubt that I became a formidable bully at a very early age. I smelled weakness and would pounce on the weakest in any group both verbally and physically. I physically fought every day till I was about nineteen when a real 'nerd' I was bullying suddenly punched me in the nose; that had never happened before. My rage had always been so extreme that no one could come near me.

A bully is a person with a strong belief in weakness and un-worthiness who needs to crush or humiliate others to have any sense of strength. Who does a bully pick on?—a person with exactly the same beliefs who has chosen a different way in which to experience those beliefs. Surely it is clear by now that punishing bullies will not make the slightest difference; on the contrary, punishment is what a bully is looking for. He believes he is bad and evil, and deserves to be punished. I was punished constantly by my father and at school, kicked out of class on a daily basis; that is what my ego was looking for and received. Unless we start bringing the victim and the victimizer together and have them see that they are the same—that they have identical beliefs and that both just desperately want love—nothing will change. This is not about behavior modification. Yes, the bully has to stop his aggressive behavior, but that is just the very first step. Then the actual transformation of beliefs has to begin.

Depression

There is little doubt that depression has become an epidemic or even pandemic condition of our time. A few minutes of research will show you the staggering percentage of our population now on anti-depressants or illegal drugs. Why is that? Could it be that many of us have accepted the devastating judgment of ourselves the ego dictates daily? Could it be that we experience a literal starvation of real love, and have lost sight of any real purpose to be alive? Could it also be that the relentless marketing machines, telling us that if we only bought this or that product we would be happy, lead us only into a gnawing emptiness with each purchase?

The Six-Step Process presented in this writing is a very effective way to reconnect to the truth within, freeing us from all negative and limiting core beliefs.

Medicine, Health and Wellness

We briefly looked at the impact of the Six-Step Process on mental health, and it would not be too much of a challenge to grasp the potential for physical well-being as well. Look at it this way: if I knew that my worth is intrinsic—that I am Love, and innocence is at the core of my very being—would it even occur to me to drink to excess or ingest harmful chemicals of any kind? If I know who I am and I have a purpose for being, I will naturally take care of my body so that it can serve me in that purpose.

Why do health fads fail? Why do weight loss programs continue to rake in billions from repeat customers? Because they never deal with the underlying cause of over eating. In 2011-2012, 69% of adult Americans over the age of twenty were overweight or obese. That is what self-hatred will do. The social and economic costs are staggering. Once we learn to appreciate who we are in truth, the idea of harming ourselves through poor diet and health habits would be an alien one.

Attention Deficit Hyperactivity Disorder (ADHD)

Talk about an epidemic! Close to ten million kids have been diagnosed with ADHD in the US alone. We have had many individuals come to the center with that diagnosis but it never takes long to overcome it, in most cases. Having this diagnosis serves a purpose. Find out what the purpose is, decide you no longer need it, and healing begins.

One youth who could not sit still for more than just a few seconds had a belief that he was stupid. If he acted out, no one expected anything from him. A young woman come to us with 'severe' ADHD and discovered that her belief was: "I don't matter." With ADHD, she *did* matter. A shocking adjunct was that her mum, her dad, and brother—who came to the center for her last week—all had the same diagnosis and were on the same medication. How did that happen? Well, they all had the same psychiatrist. Every one of these, and so many others, are now off their ADHD meds. Here are a few steps, in addition to doing the Six-Step Process, that will help enormously with healing ADHD:

- Learn to meditate and practice it all day long.
- Cut sugar out of your diet (important regardless of whether you have ADHD or not).
- Limit your time on electronic devices.
- Exercise, go for long walks in nature.

Criminal Justice System

The U.S. now has by far the most people incarcerated (as a percentage of population) of any industrialized nation on earth. Why is that? How is it possible that we as a society still cling tenaciously to the punishment/reward system, which has proven to be so disastrous for so long? Our jails are full of guilty people. We are convinced of that. The bad news is the prison population agrees as well, at a deep level, while of course protesting their innocence.

Here is a radical suggestion: It costs over $100,000 to keep a single prisoner in jail for a year. If we were to assign one coach trained in the Six-Step Process to, say, four prisoners and paid that coach the princely salary of $100,000, society would save $300,000 each year because those four prisoners could soon safely be released. Now, I would never suggest that this process is designed to save money; it is designed to save lives. It is designed to bring dignity and love back to families and communities in distress. The reason I offered that little calculation is primarily because money makes sense to most, whereas 'spirituality' is scary.

When we start to see that spirituality and its multiple applications is not just beneficial but profitable, the world will enter the next great renaissance, and this rebirth will change the planet in ways we have never even imagined. Our jails are full of people whose foundational core belief is the belief in guilt, and whatever they did to get themselves in jail is evidence for that belief. It really is that simple.

Many years ago at a workshop, a young man admitted that he had oral sex not just with his four-year-old daughter, but also with the daughter of friends for whom he babysat. The workshop, mostly women, exploded and it took the entire length of the work-shop to process all reactions. Then we were faced with the legal reality that we had to report this to the police. We did, he was charged and a prosecutor was assigned to the case. The defendant received help from a legal aid lawyer who was re-signed to the inescapable fact that the young man would end up in jail. We have all heard horror stories of what happens in jail to sex offenders, particularly those who have victimized young children.

I contacted the prosecutor and presented a proposal of in-tensive daily therapy for a year. I explained that this young man had sought out the worst evidence he could create to support his belief in unworthiness—to the extreme that he, himself, be-lieved he deserved to die. The prosecutor was intrigued by my presentation and my client became the first man in the legal system with his offence not to be sent to jail. Now, fifteen years later, he is well adjusted. His child and the other little girl have received ample counseling. A life was saved and a family was given another chance at a harmonious, healing experience.

Happiness Quotient

If I accept that my one and only purpose for being on the planet is to be happy, than it follows that I will use every situation to achieve that purpose. I have then made a conscious decision to reverse cause and effect. The ego will tell me that a situation either brings me joy or sadness, while this teaching helps me see that these emotional reactions to any situation are chosen by me. The situation does not bring me joy or sadness; it is my interpretation of it that does so. Marcus Aurelius said: "If you are distressed by anything external, the pain is not due to the thing itself, but to your estimate of it; and this you have the power to revoke at any moment." Choose Again, in other words.

Sports

It was my privilege to play sports at a fairly high level, on national teams and in top divisions. I played to humiliate the opposition (remember the bully?) and I had some talent. I can only dream of having the body that I had fifty years ago and play with the joy that I would now experience playing. This process has the potential to bring the words "play" and "game" back into sports. I can only imagine what it would feel like to stand over a three foot putt without the slightest fear, without even a hint of the insane idea that my worth would be established by sinking it or missing it. I have often thought that we could virtually guarantee a two- or three-point drop in the handicap of any golfer practicing this process.

More relevant to most of us, how would our kids feel if they learned to play sports because it was fun? The idea that you might lose, and still have an absolute blast playing a game—do our kids ever learn that?

Business

There are many who work at a job they hate to make money to buy things they don't need. If you recognize yourself in that rather bleak description, this process may just turn your life up-side down at first—but then you will experience a terrific surge of joy. The most surprising aspect is that you may very well continue to do the same job, but now derive immense satisfaction from it. You see, it is not about the job but about purpose! As we saw above, if my purpose is to be happy, then the workplace will be a happy place. And the ripple effect of having a foolproof conflict resolution process in the workplace is immeasurable. With the Six-Step Process all so-called 'conflicts' are neutralized and resolved. First the conflict is stripped of its emotional content, and then the process takes us to the essence of the disagreement, which is a choice between neutral facts. It takes the emotion out of boardroom negotiations. It takes the sting out of strife and inter-competition. It opens the door to clearly seeing what is in the highest and best interest of all. It allows a real possibility for a win-win workplace. That has to be worth a try!

Families and Relationships

Whenever a couple under stress comes to see me, the first question I ask is: "What is the purpose of your relationship?" It may come as a surprise that they never have an answer other than the predictable... *uh, we love each other ... we have two kids to raise... we have a mortgage to pay off.* I will put it very simply here: the purpose for any relationship is to heal old, limiting core beliefs. The purpose is to lovingly be there for each other whenever one is temporarily insane, reminding each other of what is the truth. By insane, I mean that one of us believes something that is not true. All relationships are ultimately either with the 'self' or with the 'Self'. I have attracted my partner because she is an unfailing mirror for my insanities. She and I have the same beliefs and will trigger each other in order to correct beliefs.

To recognize that my happiness does not come from my partner, to acknowledge that I do not have the faintest idea what love is, and then to look at all that stands in the way of seeing my partner as who she really is and remove those barriers— that is the real purpose of any relationship. I have to know that I am whole and complete and do not 'need' my partner, and vice versa. And then I have to also know that I am not always aware of that truth, and what prevents me from knowing who I am are a few mistaken beliefs. Once I accept the joyful fact that the relationship is a crucible designed to burn out all impurities (read: mistaken beliefs), then the relationship shifts from a battleground to a joyful lab for healing.

Divorce

So often when we work with young adults and teenagers, we find that one of the most traumatic events they've experienced is the divorce of their parents. Why is that? Children invariably take on full responsibility for the divorce. It seems to be their fault that their parents weren't happy, and split up. This conviction contains the underlying message that divorce is a bad thing. However, with proper counseling, this message or belief can be reframed so that a "failed" marriage is seen to be what it really is: part of a growth cycle on the part of everyone involved. Good counseling enables people to leave their marriage in a loving manner instead of parting in an acrimonious way. Unfortunately, this kind of counseling is not typical in our culture today, but if it were, children would be more apt to view the circumstance of divorce with more objectivity and not as much guilt.

Public Speaking

The prospect of having to speak in public is widely dreaded.

This is not just an emotional matter, as it may affect one's professional standing. Fear of public speaking fear has a 10% impairment on wages; a 10% impairment on college graduation; and a 15% impairment on promotion to management. These are significant factors. Perhaps the best way to illustrate how the Six-Step Process can help is to tell a story of my own.

When I got married in 1969, it was necessary to make a speech. I had never spoken in public and when I rose to address the family and friends gathered, I managed to squeeze out "Thank you" before my throat seized up. No more words were forthcoming. I was literally paralyzed with fear. In 1989, at my second wedding, I was more ready. I started and managed to expand on the address I delivered twenty years earlier: "Thank you all for coming." A vast improvement, but the same paralysis set in. Fast forward to practicing the Six Steps and processing the beliefs that prevented me from uttering a co-herent sentence. I now speak in public at many venues worldwide, often for an hour and a half without notes. How did that happen? I healed the beliefs that choked my throat. Anyone can do this.

Sexual Harassment

> *"The word 'innocence' means a mind that is incapable of being hurt."* ~ KRISHNAMURTI

This subject was very much in the news in 2017 and will likely draw attention for years to come. If society is finally ready to move away from the fatiguing paradigm of victim vs. victimizer and surrender the urge to punish the victimizer, well then, perhaps we can make some real progress in this systemic challenge. As we discussed earlier, punishment has never worked. For a man to commit the offence of inappropriate sexual contact he would have to "objectify" women; what so many fail to recognize is that in order to objectify women, the same must have been done to the perpetrator long before. The root cause lies in the alienation of 'other', that is, the deep experience of separation. Thus it is separation that needs to be healed, and that will happen only when we recognize that victim and victimizer are inextricably linked and both deserve a process of deep healing. Punishing the victimizer is not the answer. Please, remember we are never talking about condoning 'bad' behaviour but simply offering an answer to a societal problem by going after the root cause rather than the symptom.

Consumerism

There was a store in Vancouver many years ago that had the most honest advertising I have ever seen: "Don't need it? We got it!" What is behind the rampant consumerism we are now witnessing—seven-year-olds with iPads, ten-year-olds with smart-phones? What is this endless craving for more? The ego always wants more. More toys, yes, but also more suffering, more special traumas, more of anything. What the Six-Step Process will help us do is look into the underlying cause of this hunger. The driving force behind consumerism is a belief that something, anything from outside of me will bring me what I want. Yet true happiness means having no desires!

As you can gather by now, there really is no area of your life where diligent application of the Six-Step process will not have a dramatic impact. Make a commitment to yourself today to take full ownership of everything in your life, and at the same time commit to the teaching that everything is for the Self that we all share, and the world will become a better place.

Gratitudinal Expressions

YEARS AGO, at a European conference of Transpersonal Psychology in Milan where I was invited to speak, I was asked who my teachers were. The answer is: You. All who came to me for counseling, all who came to our center to heal an old hurt or ancient wound, all who will read this book and change their lives while affecting untold others... You are my teachers.

Now, to be a little more specific: The Six-Step Process is a natural progression from a process my first teacher, Sandy Levey-Lunden, taught in the first ACIM workshops I took with her in 1993. It was her conviction, passion and commitment that gave me the courage to undergo my own great undoing of beliefs. It was Suzi Butterfield in Arenal (CR) who told me I was a 'therapist' when that idea was so far from my mind. Dr. Gerald Jampolsky convinced me, finally, to write this book. Jerry and Diane Cirincione graciously agreed to write the foreword and then, it was Gerard Krans who provided the financial support needed for lift off. Without Stan and Jane Silverman's unfailing trust in our work so much of what we, and others, have been able to do for so many would not have been possible.

Anne Dillon wrote an early draft, and Anne Andrew added to it, conceived the structure of the book and nudged me to keep going. Anne's loving persistence ensured that we now can offer you a blueprint of a most useful and practical path to inner peace.

Gratitude is due to the Choose Again staff and friends: Elaine Clark, Christie Dakin, Saskia Wolsak, Diane Rice, Dawn Cleland Green, Sarah Kopinya, Claudette Thomas, Fred Wilberts,

Paul Panteleyev, Andrew Burt, Andrea Stihl, Dr. David Vass, Amy Rice, Sean Smith, Dr. Dennis Gaither, Lissa Wolsak, Dr. Norma Clark, Claire Shannon, Dr.Christine Walters, Veronica Dahl, Greg Lynch, Dave Vass, Gila Golub, Dr. Gabor Maté, Eric Andrew, Fritha Wolsak, Dr. Rodolfo Roth, Angela Roth, Dr. Richard Pollay, Christine Riedtmann, Dr. Carole Christopher, Martin Engi, Dr. Brent Haskell, Fred Matser, Marvin Egberts, Dick Woudenberg, and so many others, too many to mention, played key roles in the development of the material in this book. Each one of you is an inspiration to so many!

D. Patrick Miller very quickly realized the importance of this little book and became the agent, or patient doula, providing invaluable insight and guidance.

Every night at our center we end the day with rounds of Gratitude. Now it is my turn and this gratitude reaches out to All of You. My final Gratitude is for Stacy Sully, my noble reflection, who gently teaches me how to love every day.

APPENDIX A

Feelings Sheet

The following list is an extensive, but certainly not exhaustive compilation of thoughts, attitudes and emotions that may characterize your experience.

Abandoned
Agony
Afraid
Alone
Angry
Anxious
Apprehensive
Ashamed
At a loss
Betrayed
Blame
Bored
Burdened
Cheated
Concerned
Confused
Crazy
Crushed
Cornered
Defeated
Defensive
Dejected
Depressed
Despair
Despondent
Devastated
Disappointed
Discouraged
Disgusted
Dismayed
Disoriented
Doubting

Embarrassed
Empty
Emptiness
Enraged
Exhausted
Fatigued
Fearful
Heartache
Heartbroken
Heartsick
Helpless
Humiliated
Horror
Horrified
Inadequate
Indifferent
Indignant
Invalidated
Lazy
Lethargic
Lonely
Loss
Lost
Mad
Melancholy
Mortified
Offended
Outraged
Overwhelmed
Persecuted
Pressured
Punished

Put Down
Put Upon
Rage
Rebellious
Rejected
Rejecting
Resentment
Sadness
Deep Sadness
Scared
Scorn
Self-conscious
Shame
Shattered
Silly
Sorrow
Deep Sorrow
Suffering
Suspicious
Terror
Tired
Tortured
Trapped
Traumatized
Uncertain
Unsafe
Untrusting
Violent
Vulnerable
Wasted
Wary
Worn Out

APPENDIX B

Other Tools of Transformation

Here are some other tools of transformation that are part of the Choose Again methodology for psychological and spiritual transformation.

Gratitude

If I work one-on-one with someone who's depressed, and I say to that person, "Go home tonight and write down ten things you're grateful for," invariably their response is: "I can't think of one thing I'm grateful for."

But the truth is, anyone can. Initially, however, someone can be in so much pain that they feel they've got nothing to be grateful for.

In our residential healing practice, everyone at the communal dinner gets a chance to list the things they were grateful for that day. This nightly practice also helps people to notice, during the day, the people and events who are enriching their lives. It's exciting to watch what happens when you acknowledge what you're grateful for. Things begin to shift immediately.

True gratitude is simply recognizing that we're all One. Many people who come to us for healing don't recognize this at first, but over the course of their work, they come to understand it in a very profound way.

Meditation

Meditation doesn't necessarily mean sitting in the lotus position and saying "Ommmmm." In its true form, it means watching our thoughts at all times. When I watch and monitor my thoughts, I learn how to reframe the ones that cause me distress. If I don't catch my thoughts they tend to get out of control quickly—and when this happens, it gets harder to recognize their source.

In addition to this overarching form of meditation, there are other types that we practice. One exercise involves slowly counting backward from the number 27, silently, to oneself. This calms the mind. When you do it, you're not thinking about the fact that you didn't pay your taxes, you're not thinking about terrorists, you're not thinking about that annoying new coworker... you're simply counting. A variation on this practice is to count backward with your breathing: Breathe in for a count of five, then hold for a count of five. Breathe out for a count of five, then you hold for a count of five. And you keep doing that. You can do it while you're driving, while you're at a traffic light, while you're at the grocery store. It's a really useful, simple, and practical meditation that helps to quiet and center the mind.

Holotropic Breathwork

Holotropic Breathwork is a breathing technique introduced in the West by Dr. Stan Grof. Dr. Grof is a leading, innovative and brilliant psychiatrist and healer who used ayahuasca, mushrooms, and peyote in his practice to allow his clients to bypass their normal ego defenses. When these substances became illegal for use in therapeutic sessions, Stan Grof realized that Prana breathing might induce similar states.

The key to this breathing is to allow it to be continuous, with no break at the top or bottom of the breath. There are a variety of physical reactions that people have reported, from tingling in the hands and feet, to nausea, and even tetany, a form of involuntary muscle contraction in the hands. All these symptoms pass if one continues the breath. In this altered state, one often has access to various previously inaccessible parts of one's psyche. Once these deeply buried memories come to the surface the client often experiences a profound release.

This is a healing modality that we use frequently. I'll give you an example from my own life—something that came up after I had spent about a year turning my life around, when I was in my fifties. As you might recall, I was incarcerated in a POW camp when I was a young boy. At this point on my path, I thought I'd gotten my entire camp experience out of my system. I felt no hatred toward the camp guards; I had no lingering animosity about the experience itself. I really didn't feel anything around it. Thus I thought it was completely resolved.

But in fact, every time the subject of the camp came up in workshops or in other conversations, my throat would constrict. It became pretty clear that there was something still tied to that experience that I hadn't looked at yet.

And so I decided to apply Holotropic breathwork to this issue and within five minutes I started to howl like a wounded bull. What became clear to me was that I felt responsible for all the suffering I'd seen in the camps; I thought it was all my fault. With more breathing, I realized that I felt responsible for all the camps in the world—and then, I was responsible for the entire second World War! I was carrying around so much irrational guilt about the first three years of my life that could not have been addressed by normal cognitive approaches. I cannot imagine a therapist saying to me: "Your problem is that you feel guilty for WWII" without me walking out of the room shaking my head.

Yet, there it was: a deeply held belief in guilt which I had acted out through anger and substance abuse for fifty years. This one breathing changed my life forever!

With Holotropic Breathing, similar astounding breakthroughs have been experienced here at our center and at workshops we conduct around the world.

Exercise and Physical Catharsis

In a typical day at our residential center in Costa Rica, we have an extended healing circle in the morning that lasts for a couple of hours. These sessions can be pretty intense. After a hearty lunch, we typically encourage everyone to go on a long hike together, or we may play soccer.

It's very important to move the body in order to process the thoughts of the mind. Recently scientists have determined that undertaking bilateral activity helps to process trauma. In a normal brain, the events in our lives are stored as memories. A traumatic event, however, which is loaded with negative emotion, is apt to operate as if on a playback loop, and in so doing, remain omnipresent in one's consciousness. When we take a walk, go for a swim, play tennis, or do jumping jacks, both parts of the brain are activated because both sides of the body are in motion. Scientists have found that this engagement allows traumatic memories to become "unstuck" and properly stored in long-term memory, and thus no longer active in one's daily awareness.

In the work that we do we've long used the activities of sport to aid in the processing of trauma, so it's interesting but hardly surprising that science now corroborates our practice.

Appendix C

Testimonials

Here are some testimonials by individuals who have bene-
fited from the Choose Again Six-Step Process:

"I was a classic workaholic. My work kept me from thinking about the emptiness I felt inside... I had an outwardly perfect life—a wife and two children, a house in a desirable neighborhood, high income from a well-paying job, a member of senior
leadership in multinational professional services firm in Canada
and a well-respected member of the community. In order to maintain this façade I worked long hours at the office, and then
brought more work home every evening and at weekends. I
was chronically late home for dinner and missed my children's
school performances.

"When my children became teenagers all of the veneer started to peel off. My stress levels were through the roof and I could
not cope with the added stress of parenting teens. I blamed my
job, my co-workers, and my upbringing, and became increasingly
miserable. Fortunately I met Diederik Wolsak and spent a week
at the Choose Again Center in Costa Rica.

"In a very short time I was able to understand where my
problems were coming from, take responsibility for my experience in life, and change my way of thinking. The results of using
the Six-Step Process regularly were extraordinary. I became

happier than I ever imagined I could be. All my relationships improved tremendously—with my wife, my children, parents, friends, and clients. My stress level came down to close to zero. I was able to effortlessly take on a more senior, global position in the firm, and when a sudden reorganization occurred I was able to take it in stride—a very challenging situation for anyone. My only wish is that I could have learned these techniques sooner in my life, but better late than never!" ~ ERIC ANDREW

"Looking back at my life ten years ago, when I was first introduced to the teachings of Diederik and Choose Again and now seeing who I am today... I am so grateful for the Six-Step Process. It is a technique that has empowered me to withstand life's hardest moments with such peace, yet also allows me to fully embrace the exquisite moments of joy my life equally includes. This book offers the means to transform who we believe we are into who we are in truth...infinitely powerful and loving! Diederik and his work have truly been a gift to me and countless others and I look forward to sharing his latest publication with those who desire change in their lives." ~ DR. DAVID VASS

"I have been working with the Six-Step Process for about fifteen years now, and it has become my automatic response to my upsets. What I love about it is that it is so brilliantly clear: I am upset, my upset is about me, and I am responsible for correcting the negative belief that triggered the upset. Then I get to be happy again. Thank you for introducing this simple way of problem solving!" ~ DONNA HONE

"The Six-Step Process is an incredible tool for total life transformation and taking responsibility for one's own experience.

Before I learned how to work the Process, I had tended to "keep the crazy going" by rehashing my painful experiences, talking about them to a traditional psychotherapist. The Process gave me a powerful tool to empower myself and change the beliefs at the root of the upsets instead. It is a simple step-by-step process for identifying the underlying beliefs about oneself that are subconsciously triggered by various circumstances that one encounters. One is then empowered to "choose again." To literally choose new beliefs about oneself that are in alignment with who each of us is on the deepest level (Spirit, whole, infinite, one with all of life and Source)." ~ SHARON CHEN

"Diederik Wolsak's Choose Again Process has single-handedly changed the way I handle every upset that comes my way. Before learning this technique, I would ruminate over things constantly, viciously caught up in self loathing. Now, if I get stuck, I go through the Six Steps and remember the truth of who I am, which is pure love. This process really is the way out of all suffering. Thank you Diederik." ~ JUDY MORTON

"Last week I had a school program with 25 kids about the age of 12. A boy told me that no one liked him. He had no friends and only felt safe behind the computer. I asked him "Who is choosing to be like this?" and his answer was, "I am." Then I asked when he had felt like this for the first time. After a while he said his parents always called him a nerd when he was little. I asked him what he started to believe about himself, and he said, "I am worthless." I asked if the class believed that and everyone said no. I asked him what the truth must be. "I am valuable," and the whole group confirmed that it was the truth. I asked him how he felt now and he said: "I'm crying inside with happiness." Thank you so much Diederik! ~ TAMARA HILLEBRANDT

"The Six Step Process was for me a key missing link. I was intellectually a proficient and curious student of metaphysics, but I learned you got to feel it to heal it. Also, I was increasingly able to gain a holographic experience utilizing the Six Step Process, especially in The Circle in Costa Rica. Having learned the body is a neutral communication tool for the Higher Self, but never having experienced such a thing, the Six Step Process with The Circle culminated in the experience of feeling infinite waves of Love pulsating through my heart chakra. It was a glimpse into the Truth of me, a very direct experience. Deep gratitude, for I believe the Six Step Process helped facilitate what has been for me a healing process." ~ Sunny Yoon

"I was at a low point in my life when I first attended a Choose Again five-day workshop in 2011. It's fair to say that the teachings and methodology offered in the Six Step Process had a profoundly positive and transformative effect on the course of my life. So helpful has this practical process been that in my role as a secondary school counsellor, I routinely teach the Six Step Process to students who are amazed by both the simplicity and radicalness of what they learn. It's like they are finally hearing what they've been longing for. These teachings will change your life as they changed mine." ~ Sean Smith

"The first thought that comes to mind when I consider the six weeks I spent at El Cielo is the love that permeates the place. No ooey-gooey kind of touchy-feely thing, the love is hard and real and worth the effort. The love Diederik and his staff practice is grueling work. Peeling back years of self-deception, and discovering who you are is as terrifying as it is bliss-filled, by no stretch of the imagination an easy job. Besides possessing a heart as big as all outdoors, Diederik's rapier wit insures that no one spends much time wallowing in a morass of self-pity. A trailblazer in this frontier of self-discovery, he uses his six steps tirelessly on himself, then brings the fruits of his labor to share in the daily therapeutic circles with any and all that have ears to hear and a heart desiring the way home." ~ MARY MORONY

"The Six Step Process is an outstanding psychospiritual tool both for resolving psychological conflicts and doing transformational work. Based on the assumption that every human being is intrinsically loving and beloved, the Six Step Process helps to uncover the resistances to this state of being. The resistance is based on unconscious beliefs. In principle this process is simple, but there is a certain discipline needed to apply it in daily life. Since this discipline became part of my psychospiritual exercising, my levels of joy, love, and vitality have increased considerably. I wish everyone on this planet could come to know this excellent method of inner growth and wealth." ~ DR. RODOLFO ROTH

"Diederik's pioneering work, process, and unconditional love has helped me to regain and sustain my original state of heart and mind." ~ SIMON REILLY, Leading Advisor Inc.

"I found Diederik on YouTube and practiced the six steps alone for a few months before doing a week's retreat in France with him. For me the process has been mind and life changing. The Six Step method is a direct, quick way of identifying and healing old beliefs which keep us from knowing who we really are, which is love. I can say it's the most effective healing process I've ever done. It can be challenging work at times as old beliefs can be stuck but I've found, with willingness to heal, it gets easier. I am so grateful for this teaching as I feel more peace and joy in my life. I don't sweat the small stuff anymore! With eternal thanks to your dedication to heal Diederik as you heal us all with you!" ~ ANGELA CLOCHERTY

"I never entertained the thought that the truth of who I am is pure love until I started attending the Choose Again Circles and several of the workshops. It was unfamiliar to me. It has been a great gift that gives me much more peace and joy in my life. I am truly grateful to those at Choose Again for the work they are doing. With gratitude." ~ LESLIE VANDER HAEGEN

"I had the blessed opportunity to be at one of your circle gatherings in BC a few years ago. I embraced your Six Steps immediately because my mind was able to grasp it so easily. Whenever I get triggered I am able to stop the negative judgements by telling myself that "the feeling is in me". That step is my favourite because it reminds me that I am responsible for how I feel, and my upset is caused by me and nobody else. I then feel the freedom and empowerment. It reminds me that I have the power and the choice is mine in deciding the quality of the moment. Thank you D for your simple, powerful, and life-enhancing teachings." ~ GERI SAVAGE

"I was first introduced to the work through daily emails and YouTube. I was inspired by the video titled Relationships and Marriage to attend a week-long retreat to go deeper. I had never experienced spiritual work that could not only diffuse an upset quickly, but also beautifully designed to realign me to the truth of my being. I have been practicing and sharing the Six Steps for 4 years and it truly is a simple process to return home to freedom anytime I choose." ~ SANDY SHULER

"I struggled with alcoholism, severe depression and couldn't find a way out of the continuous dark story I was telling myself. Never have I encountered a more effective process in dealing with core beliefs and how they shape my view of the world. Choose the loving thing to do and you will experience miracles." ~ NATHAN MARKEE

"Authentic! Authentic! Authentic! This is not instant trans-formation. Being a cook, I think of this process as taking off one layer of the phyllo dough darkening my mind each time I use it. I have a lifetime of 'cooking' ahead of me." ~ DIANNE WESTFALL

"I met Diederik in 2012 after struggling with depression for years—a byproduct of my Type A personality where good was never close to good enough. His insight and the Six Step process changed my life and taught me that if I'm ever upset, I have the choice to change my mind about whatever I think is preventing me from feeling at peace. As a result, I'm happier in my relationships with my family and friends, I'm a better, more loving parent, and ironically, I'm more effective at work. Diederik is one of the most profound teachers I've ever known and I'm grateful for the impact he has had on my life." ~ DANIEL ANDREW

"From someone who often couldn't resist the temptation, at times even felt an urge to engage in intellectual skirmishes with you, whom you sometimes called your twin brother (because of that?), and who to this day can't get himself to fully assimilate the "I am / You are Love, thank God that is the Truth" line, I have to admit that the concept of taking full authorship of whatever I may feel has radically changed my outlook on life and those that I engage with, and where my still haphazard and not always wholly successful attempts at applying this has and continues to

change my emotional well-being. For the better..."
~ Love, TOBIAS

"This process and work has saved my life and sanity. Since I started my conscious process of healing over 15 years ago, this has been the most transformative journey I have had so far—because it continues as an ongoing invitation to return to Love and Self all the time. I have shared this process with those who are interested and will continue doing so as I see the miracles that are unfolding in my life. A true gift!

"I am so grateful that Spirit has led me to the process and how my vision has changed since then and continues to open to more and more beauty and goodness. My intention for this work is that it touches as many souls open to true radical transformation as possible so that Spirit can do the work through us. As I go along, I trust that my deepening will allow me one day to bring this to the younger generations to support a guilt-free and joyful life! May the work flourish and expand.... !" ~ PRIYA BEATE LAASCH

"For me personally, it was a big 'awakening' that at the core of my being, who I am is; perfect, whole and complete. And, although I'd been studying Vedic philosophy, psychology, Yoga and Buddhist teachings and many practices of self help and healing over many years, the Choose Again work and Six Step process helped me solidify and live this truth from an awaken heart. There is still work to do, and I am humble and grateful for it. The Six Step process is the easiest, most effective process that I personally have ever used and shared. Within a few minutes any upset and conflict I am experiencing becomes an opportunity for health and healing and is for me. It's actually quite exciting as I pull back the layers of beliefs, habits, behaviours, and addictions and see truth. I am Love. From my heart." ~ TARA PILLING

"Not to get all mushy about it, but Diederik and El Cielo changed my life. Step Two of the Six Step process ("it's all about me") annoyed me right from the start. But ultimately, it's the most important one. Seeing that it was my responses to things that were driving me nuts — rather than the things themselves — was tremendously helpful. It provided a way in to look at deep, deep stuff. The daily circles at El Cielo also are very powerful. Watching other people go through the process of wrestling with their heaviest issues as Diederik drills down (which can take 45 minutes) helped me to see the commonalities in all our struggles. Thanks Diederik!" ~ MICHAEL CHURCHILL

"I discovered the Six Steps on YouTube and immediately sensed the potential. It became almost like a mantra for me and I got to the point where I could run the Six Steps in my mind with great ease. Then I began using it with people I am coaching and found that it works just as well for others. I have experienced a lot of new-found peace that was missing in my life. And, I know this process will be a part of my life and work from now on. Many thanks to Diederik for generously sharing this powerful trans-formational tool." ~ DAVID CHARD, President, EngagingMinds

APPENDIX D

Recommended Reading

- *I AM THAT*, talks with Sri Nisargadatta Maharaj.
- *Love is Letting Go of Fear* by Gerald Jampolsky
- *Healing the Addictive Mind* by Lee Jampolsky
- *The Power of Now* by Eckhart Tolle
- *This* by H. W. L. Poonja
- *The Yoga Sutras of Patanjali*
- *The Brain That Changes Itself* by Norman Doidge, MD
- *Writings of Ramana Maharshi*
- *A Return to Love* by Marianne Williamson
- *Spiritual Emergency* by Christina and Stanislov Grof
- *Mindfulness In Plain English* by Gunaratana
- *Journey Beyond Words* by Brent Haskell
- *The Soul of Rumi* or any book by Rumi
- The writings of Meister Eckhart
- *Wake up and Roar* by H. W. L. Poonja
- *Take me to Truth* by Nouk Sanchez/Tomas Vieira
- *Handbook to Higher Consciousness* by Ken Keyes
- *Man's Search for Meaning* by Viktor Frankl
- *Sex, Ecology, Spirituality* by Ken Wilber
- *A New Earth* by Eckhart Tolle
- *Molecules of Emotion* by Candice Pert
- *The Black Butterfly* by Richard Moss
- *Addiction as a Spiritual Journey* by Christina Grof
- *Manifest Your Destiny* by Wayne Dyer
- *Fire in the Soul* and *Guilt is the Teacher, Love is the Lesson* by Joan Borysenko

- *Man Enough* by Frank Pittman
- *How to Know God* by Deepak Chopra
- *Touching Spirit Bear* by Ben Mikaelsen
- *Education of Little Tree* by Forrest Carter
- *The Empty Chair* by Rebbe Nachman of Breslov
- *My Stroke of Insight* by Jill Bolte Taylor, Ph.D.
- *A Course in Understanding and Acceptance* by Regina Dawn Akers
- *You are the Placebo* by Joe Dispenza
- *In the Realm of Hungry Ghosts* by Gabor Maté MD
- *When the Body Says No* by Gabor Maté MD
- *The Work* by Byron Katie
- *A Course in Miracles*, Standard Edition published by The Foundation for Inner Peace